Now You're Talking! ^3

Strategies for Conversation

JEANNETTE D. BRAGGER

JANET SOLBERG

NATIONAL
GEOGRAPHIC
LEARNING | HEINLE
CENGAGE Learning·

Australia • Brazil • Japan • Korea • Mexico • Singapore • Spain • United Kingdom • United States

Now You're Talking! 3
Strategies for Conversation
Jeannette D. Bragger and Janet Solberg

Publisher: Sherrise Roehr

Executive Editor: Laura Le Dréan

Acquisitions Editor: Tom Jefferies

Development Editor: Michael Poor,
Jennifer I. Carlson

Director of Global Marketing: Ian Martin

Academic Marketing Manager: Emily Stewart

Product Marketing Manager: Anders Bylund

Director of Content and Media Production:
Michael Burggren

Senior Content Project Manager:
Maryellen E. Killeen

Associate Content Project Manager:
Mark Rzeszutek

Manufacturing Manager: Marcia Locke

Senior Manufacturing Buyer:
Mary Beth Hennebury

Cover Design: PreMediaGlobal

Cover Image: M.L. Campbell/Getty Images

Interior Design: PreMediaGlobal

Composition: PreMediaGlobal

For product information and technology assistance, contact us at
Cengage Learning Customer & Sales Support, 1-800-354-9706

For permission to use material from this text or product,
submit all requests online at **cengage.com/permissions**
Further permissions questions can be emailed to
permissionrequest@cengage.com

Library of Congress Control Number: 2012947882

ISBN-13: 978-1-111-35058-1

National Geographic Learning
20 Channel Center Street
Boston, MA 02210
USA

Cengage Learning is a leading provider of customized learning solutions with office locations around the globe, including Singapore, the United Kingdom, Australia, Mexico, Brazil, and Japan. Locate your local office at
international.cengage.com/region

Cengage Learning products are represented in Canada by Nelson Education, Ltd.

Visit National Geographic Learning online at **ngl.cengage.com**

Visit our corporate website at **www.cengage.com**

Instructors: Please visit **login.cengage.com** and log in to access instructor-specific resources.

Printed in the United States of America
1 2 3 4 5 6 7 15 14 13 12

Table of Contents

TO THE INSTRUCTOR

Introduction

Now You're Talking! is a three-level English conversation series (listening and speaking) designed for courses at the intermediate level (low-intermediate to high-intermediate). The program's particular approach to conversation is based on communicative strategies applied to a variety of contexts and topics.

This approach takes into account the varying linguistic levels of students in a typical class. The program systematically encourages them to activate their prior knowledge of vocabulary and grammatical structures in the context of face-to-face interactions based on real-life communicative situations.

Now You're Talking! consistently uses communicative strategies to help students learn and solidify high-frequency phrases, reactivate vocabulary, and add to their lexical repertoire. Students will find that their conversation skills spiral upward in more complex ways as they progress through the three-level program.

Challenges of the intermediate level and the *Now You're Talking!* solutions

Typically, the intermediate range of proficiency presents two major challenges for classroom instruction in listening and speaking.

1. Varying linguistic skills

Students arrive with a variety of abilities, skills, exposure time, and background in English. Most significantly, at each phase of learning, these students have added more and more language (vocabulary, grammar, etc.) with little time to reactivate, integrate, and solidify what they learned previously. Eventually, they are all classified as intermediate users of English and find themselves working together in the same classrooms.

The *Now You're Talking!* Solution

Now You're Talking! is designed to help "organize" the English that students already know and to do so in interactions with each other. Each chapter begins by asking students to reactivate and note previously learned English. Later in the chapter, they compare their lists of words and phrases with those of other classmates. In this way, they remind themselves of what they already know and also learn new ways of expressing themselves from other students and the instructor.

Imagine this approach as a spiral. At the bottom of the spiral, students **reactivate** previously learned material. Moving upward on the spiral, they **integrate** new information with what is known. Finally, as they move to the next segment of the spiral, they **solidify** listening and speaking skills with practice in structured and open-ended activities based on authentic real-life situations. Unlike the linear "add-on" approach used in so many other series, *Now You're Talking!* gives students time to work at their own level with regularity and to organize their communicative skills before being asked to move upward again.

2. The nature of conversation

Often in classroom settings, the short exchanges that involve single questions and answers are confused with conversations. In addition, students are often told what to say and how to say it. While such exchanges may be useful practice for newly learned grammar and vocabulary, they cannot be considered "conversing." Conversations are relatively complex segments of discourse that usually involve multiple communicative strategies. If students are limited mostly to structured and controlled activities, their ability to be involved in real-life conversations is, by extension, also limited.

Students may know some communicative strategies, but they may not necessarily have learned to combine them in unpredictable and open-ended situations. They may know a great deal of vocabulary while lacking the strategies that help them make sense of the isolated words. As a result, many students are left behind in multi-party conversations that feature authentic speech, utterances of various lengths, topic changes, hesitations, repetitions, overlapping speech, muddled enunciation, accent variations, ambient noise, and so forth.

The *Now You're Talking!* Solution

In *Now You're Talking!* students will enhance their conversational skills by

- listening to speech samples that simulate, to the extent possible, **authentic speech**. The listening strategies and activities guide students in such a way that they become quickly accustomed to the speech that they encounter in real-life situations.
- activating language systematically before they enter into conversations (**preparation**).
- focusing on the **communicative strategies** that enable them to assemble isolated words in ways appropriate to the contexts and topics. These strategies are used in a wide variety of contexts and are recycled on a regular basis.
- integrating what they have learned in controlled activities into **open-ended, less predictable conversations**. At this integrative point, the various aids and guides are withdrawn, and students must find ways to cope successfully in conversations that are very likely to occur in daily life.

Most day-to-day, non-technical conversations by native speakers are conducted at what might be termed the "intermediate" level. Therefore, students of English at the intermediate level probably already have many of the pieces needed to participate in such conversations. The challenge is to help them put the pieces together so that they can, in fact, be successful and more secure in their interactions with other speakers of English. It is this "putting together" that is the main goal of this conversation series.

Now You're Talking! Program Structure

The program has three levels.

Student Books

- Each book begins with a preliminary chapter followed by eight chapters and a speaker's handbook of communicative phrases.
- Each chapter is divided into two parts and ends with a cumulative "Improvise" section.

Schematic Chapter Outline

Part 1
  Prepare: Pre-listening, Listening, Communicative Strategies, Practice Activities
  Talk: Speaking Activities (pairs, small groups, whole class)

Part 2
  Prepare: Listening Comprehension (Listening Strategy), Communicative Strategies, Practice Activities
  Talk: Speaking Activities (whole class, pairs, small groups)

Improvise
  Cumulative listening and speaking activities, Internet activity

- Each chapter also contains three "floating" features that spin off from the chapter content and appear where logically useful to students:
  Language Focus: Highlights a grammatical structure or a lexical issue.
  Professional Context: Highlights the communicative strategies or linguistic behaviors appropriate in professional settings (business, academia).
  Cultural Connections: Highlights cultural topics about the United States as they relate to the chapter's communicative strategies. Students are asked to make comparisons with their own cultures.
- Each chapter contains a variety of activity types, from controlled practice to semi-controlled practice to open-ended activities. As deemed necessary, activities are supported by models.
- Chapter content is supported by art, photos, and realia.

Audio Program

- Each Student Book has a corresponding Student CD containing the audio materials. Complete audio scripts appear in the Student Book after Chapter 8.
- Audio recordings strive for authentic, natural speech.

Instructor's Guide

An Instructor's Guide for each level includes

- chapter summaries (content, grammar, vocabulary, communicative strategies)
- activity management (small group, whole class, etc.)
- suggestions for brainstorming activities
- suggestions for follow-up activities
- activity cards
- answers keys
- testing and evaluation techniques

Summary

Books 1 through 3 of *Now You're Talking!* generally progress as indicated in the chart below. Recycling, repetition, and spiraling upward of both speaking/listening strategies and topics are integral to the series.

Book 1	Book 2	Book 3
low-intermediate to intermediate	→	intermediate to high-intermediate
communicative strategies to topics	→	topics to communicative strategies
immediate environment	→	turning outward, toward the world
familiar	→	less familiar, but not unknown
sentences / multiple sentences (shorter discourse)	→	multiple sentences / paragraphs (longer discourse)
concrete	→	concrete / abstract
high-frequency	→	high- to lower-frequency

TO THE STUDENT

Now You're Talking! teaches you how to participate actively in conversations. You already know a lot of vocabulary. Now you'll learn the communicative strategies that help you put the words together. Communicative strategies are phrases that you need to participate appropriately in conversations. You'll learn phrases to ask for and give an opinion; phrases to ask for clarification or for more information; phrases to show your emotions; and many more. Communicative strategies help all speakers of English to communicate in real life, in real situations, with real people.

Conversation is like a ball game. A good player knows how to get the ball rolling (start a conversation), how to catch the ball (react), how and in which direction to throw the ball back (keep the conversation going), how to keep the ball in bounds (stay on topic), and how to guess other players' moves (be prepared for what others say). These strategies for how to play are as important as having the right ball and the right equipment.

Maybe you think that you don't know enough vocabulary to participate in a conversation or that your grammar is not good enough. Don't let that stop you from playing the conversation game. You probably know much more vocabulary and grammar than you realize. What you really need to learn are the **communicative strategies** to help you become a full conversational partner.

Each chapter in *Now You're Talking!* is divided into two parts. Each part starts with a **Prepare** section where you can learn communicative strategies in real conversations and practice them in activities. You "prepare" as assigned homework or in class before you're asked to interact with your classmates and your instructor. Then, you move to the **Talk** section. Here, you apply what you learned and have conversations with your classmates in pairs, small groups, or as a whole class. When you're done with the two parts, you'll do the final **Improvise** activities with your classmates. This section puts everything in the chapter together. You combine and review what you've learned, participating in conversations that you're likely to have in real life.

Most importantly, as you interact with your classmates and your instructor, be creative and have fun. Before long, you'll realize that *Now You're Talking!*

ACKNOWLEDGMENTS

I would like to thank John McHugh, who first approached me about writing an English conversation series. His initial enthusiasm was the encouragement I needed to enter into this project. My thanks also go to Sherrise Roehr and Thomas Jefferies, whose many accommodations were invaluable for the successful publication of *Now You're Talking!*

But most importantly, I reserve my profoundest gratitude for my editor, Michael Poor. His calm and patient approach to problems, his sense of humor, his willingness to ask questions in order to understand, his intelligence and willingness to argue, and his ability to navigate among sometimes conflicting points of view made him one of the very best editors I've worked with over the last 35 years. *Now You're Talking!* would not have seen the light of day if it had not been for Mike.

My thanks also to the following educators who provided invaluable feedback throughout the development of *Now You're Talking!*

Reviewers

Michael Chrzanowski
Community College of Denver

Jerry R. Kottom
Community College of Denver

April M. Darnell
University of Dayton IEP

Sheryl Meyer
English Language Center, University of Denver

Nancy Hamadou
Pima Community College

Anouchka Rachelson
Miami Dade College

Gail Kellersberger
University of Houston-Downtown

Scott C. Welsh
Arizona State University

DEDICATION

I dedicate *Now You're Talking!* to my friend and co-author, Donald Rice, who passed away in March 2010. He was excited about the prospect of writing this series. I think he would have been happy with the result.

Jeannette Bragger

PRELIMINARY CHAPTER
An English Conversation Class
"What do you like to do for fun?"

Strategies for Communication

Part 1: How to Participate in Conversations
Part 2: How to Talk about People

●● PREPARE ●●

INTRODUCTION: *What Is a Conversation?*

- A conversation is a verbal exchange that involves at least two people.
- It includes vocabulary, communicative strategies, grammar, an awareness of social contexts, and other aspects of language.

A. PRE-LISTENING First day of class. Read each conversation fragment and answer the questions that follow.

Sammy: Hey, Carlos. How's it going?

Carlos: I'm doing great, Sammy. How about you?

Sammy: Yeah, me too. It's cool that we're in this class together.

1. Have Sammy and Carlos met before? Yes _____ No _____

2. How do you know that your answer to question 1 is correct?

_____

Monica: Hi, I'm Monica.

Ahmed: Hi, Monica. Nice to meet you. I'm Ahmed. Is this the first English class you're taking here?

Monica: Yes. I transferred this semester. Have you had this teacher before?

Ahmed: Yeah. I had him for another class last semester.

3. What does Ahmed do to keep the conversation going once he's met Monica?

_____

4. Which of the two students is new to the college? _____

5. Why might you think that Ahmed likes the teacher of this class?

_____

Laura:	Hey, Soon-yi. We haven't seen each other since Professor Stockton's English class last year. So, what are you up to? Oh! I want you to meet Blanca. We just introduced ourselves to each other.
Soon-yi:	Hi Blanca. Nice to meet you. Well, my big news is that Hwan and I got married.
Laura:	No kidding! Congratulations! The three of us used to hang out together after class, Blanca.
Blanca:	Congratulations, Soon-yi. Is Hwan also going to take this class?
Soon-yi:	No. He's taking a course in computer science. But you'll meet him at our class party at the end of the semester.

6. Who is a good listener in this conversation?

_____

7. Why do you think she listens rather than talking a lot?

_____

8. Approximately when did Soon-yi and Hwan get married? How do you know?

_____

Professor:	Hi everybody. My name is Professor Maciejewski, but you can just call me Professor M.
Ahmed:	Hey, Professor M. Did you finish building your boat?
Professor:	No, I'm still working on it. What's happening with you, Ahmed?
Ahmed:	Not much. I'm still working on my English.
Professor:	I'm glad to hear that. Now let's all meet each other.

9. Why do you think everyone calls the teacher "Professor M"?

_____

10. What else do we find out about Professor M?

_____

11. What do you think about Ahmed's question right after Professor M introduces himself to the class?

_____

B. LISTENING Nice to meet you. Listen to the conversation between Professor M and one of the new students in the English conversation class. Then fill in the chart with the topics covered and the questions or comments used to keep the conversation going.

TOPICS	QUESTIONS / COMMENTS TO KEEP THE CONVERSATION GOING

CD 1 🔊 **C.** LISTENING Let's introduce ourselves. On the first day of English class, Professor M
Tracks asks students to introduce themselves. Listen to the introductions and complete the
3–6 chart. Write *NI* in the spaces where no information is available about that topic.

1. Write the information each student provides.

	PLACE OF ORIGIN	FAMILY	STUDIES	WORK	FUTURE PLANS	LEISURE TIME
Zahid						
Mariana						
Li Ming						
Chul-Soo						

2. For each introduction, write two follow-up questions you could ask the person if you were in a conversation with him or her.

Zahid

_____

_____

Mariana

_____

_____

Li Ming

_____

_____

Chul-Soo

_____

_____

COMMUNICATIVE STRATEGIES: _How to Participate in Conversations_

Miki: So, Shen, what do you like to do when you're, um … not studying?

Hakim: I go to the movies a lot … or I watch them on my computer.

Miki: I really like movies too. What ah … what kinds do you like?

Hakim: Um … I like science fiction … and also comedies.

Miki: What do you mean by science fiction?

Hakim: Well … I like movies that take place in the future or in space … like _Star Wars_.

Miki: Yes, I like that too. They are … ah … easy to understand. But American comedies are difficult because I don't understand English too well. So … I don't always know if something is funny.

Hakim: I know what you mean. But I think that watching movies is one of the best ways to learn English.

Miki: That's probably true. It's like watching television. I learn a lot from television. But I still think it's important to take this class.

Hakim: Definitely.

Starting Conversations

With Someone You Don't know

Hello / Hi, …

I'm / My name is …

How are you?

(It's) nice to meet you. / Pleased to meet you.

You look familiar. Have we met before? / Do we know each other?

Let me introduce you to … / This is …

With Someone You Know

Hey, / Hi, + *name of person*

What's up? / What's new? / What's happening?

How's it going? / How are you? / How're you doing? / How are things?

What are you up to?

What have you been up to since …?

How was your summer / weekend / vacation / *etc.*?

Keeping the Conversation Going: Getting to Know Someone

Information: *yes/no questions* / who, whose, which, what, where, when, why (how come), how

Clarification: What happened (exactly)? / What do you mean? / For example? / You said that … + *follow-up question*

Repetition: Could you repeat that? / (I'm) sorry, I didn't get that. What did you say? / Sorry, what was that?

Reaction: Really? / No kidding! / Congratulations! / That's great! / That's true.

Changing the subject: By the way, + *question* / Speaking of … / Changing the subject …

Note: See the *Speaker's Handbook* on page 165 for additional phrases.

Language Focus: Conversations Among Students

Here are a few topics that you can use when you meet other students. These topics help you keep the conversation going and begin to get to know the person.

• where the person was born, is from, or has lived
• how long the person has lived here (been at this school)
• languages the person speaks
• the person's major or academic interests
• what the person likes to do when not studying
• the person's job or work
• the person's interests (movies, sports, music reading, games, TV, etc.)

You should avoid the following topics unless the other person volunteers information: family, politics, religion, health, money, physical appearance, and any other highly personal information.

D. Appropriate responses. Write an appropriate greeting for each response. Use phrases from the **Communicative Strategies.**

1. A: _____

 B: Not bad, and you?

2. A: _____

 B: Not much. I'm still working at the biology lab.

3. A: _____

 B: It's possible. Were you at the orientation meeting last weekend?

4. A: _____

 B: Hi, Pablo. Where are you from?

5. A: _____

 B: Well, let's see. After the end of classes, I went back home to Korea.

6. A: _____

    B: Friday night, I had dinner with my parents. Saturday, I went to the football game. On Sunday, I studied all day for my philosophy exam.

7. A: _____

    B: I'm good. How about you?

8. A: _____

    B: Fine, thanks. What's happening with you?

Cultural Connections: Responding to Polite Questions

When someone greets you, it's not uncommon for the person to say, "How are you?" It's important to understand that this question is not an invitation to tell the person your life story or all the good or bad things that have happened to you lately. It's simply a polite question that is a conversation filler before you move on to other topics. In response, you should give a short, positive answer and move on with the conversation. Here are some sample answers to "How are you?"

- Fine, thanks, and you?
- Not bad, thank you, and you?
- Good. What (How) about you?
- Great. And you?

Generally, complaining or bringing up depressing or sad topics can stop conversations very quickly. So keep in mind the idea of TMI (too much information) which means the person doesn't want to hear about the topic or that the topic is inappropriate (taboo).

Where you're from, how are people expected to respond to the question "How are you?" What topics are inappropriate in conversations with people you've just met?

E. Appropriate and inappropriate questions. For each statement, write down one information question that is appropriate and one that is not. Use the phrases from the **Communicative Strategies**.

    1. A: I just bought a new car.

        B: *Appropriate:* _____

           Inappropriate: _____

    2. A: My mother works for a big company.

        B: *Appropriate:* _____

           Inappropriate: _____

    3. A: I've got to remember to go vote tomorrow.

        B: *Appropriate:* _____

           Inappropriate: _____

    4. A: I feel like I'm getting old.

        B: *Appropriate:* _____

           Inappropriate: _____

5. A: I can't come to work tomorrow. My father is sick.

    B: *Appropriate:* _____

       Inappropriate: _____

6. A: I didn't do so well in my classes last semester.

    B: *Appropriate:* _____

       Inappropriate: _____

F. Keeping the conversation going. For each statement, write a follow-up question or a reaction according to the cue in parentheses. Use the phrases from the **Communicative Strategies**.

    1. I just heard that I was accepted into medical school. (reaction / information)

    _____

    _____

    2. I can't go to the movies tonight. (information / changing the subject)

    _____

    _____

    3. He said that [*mumble, mumble*]… (repetition)

    _____

    _____

    4. … and he broke his leg. (clarification)

    _____

    _____

G. What to talk about. Write down five topics that you'd like to ask your classmates about in order to get to know them better.

H. Peer correction. Compare your answers to Activities D, E, and F to those of your classmates. Make corrections and additions to your answers as necessary.

I. Hi, I'm … Move around the room and talk to three different classmates you don't know very well. Using some or all of the topics you wrote down in Activity G, get to know these classmates better. They'll do the same with you. Use phrases from the **Communicative Strategies** to start the conversations and keep them going.

J. I like that too. Pair up with one classmate you haven't spoken to and introduce yourself. Then keep a conversation going with the person until you find an interest that you both have in common. Continue talking about that topic. Use phrases from the **Communicative Strategies**.

Example: (after the introductions)

A: *I really like American movies. What about you?*

B: *Um … I'm not crazy about movies. But you said that you really like sports. What's your favorite sport?*

A: *Soccer.*

B: *Wow! That's my favorite sport too. Do you watch it on TV? Are you on a team? …*

K. Where I'm from… Talk to your classmates about the place where you're from originally (or where your family is from). Your classmates will react appropriately, ask you follow-up questions to get clarification or more information, or change the subject. Use phrases from the **Communicative Strategies**.

Example: A: *My family and I just moved here from Venezuela.*

B: *Where in Venezuela?*

A: *The capital, Caracas.*

C: *Where exactly is Venezuela?*

A: *Well, it's on the northern coast of South America. Brazil is our neighbor on the south and Colombia is on the west.*

D: *What language do you speak in Venezuela? …*

Part Two

●● PREPARE ●●

LISTENING COMPREHENSION: *Listening Attentively*

If you want to be an active participant in a conversation, first you need to listen for key information. Then show your interest by reacting, asking for clarification or additional information, and making your own contributions to the conversation. Careful listening means that you do the following:

- Listen for key words and ignore less important ones.
  - **A:** *I really **like animals.***
  - **B:** *Me too. Do you have any pets?*
  - **A:** *I have **a dog.** He's terrific.*
  - **B:** *What's his name?*
  - **A:** ***Loki.** I named him after a god in Norse mythology.*

- Listen for topics that continue to be emphasized by the speaker.
  - **B:** *Oh, I'm really interested in Norse mythology.*
  - **A:** *I take **Loki** everywhere with me. **He's my best friend.***
  - **B:** *What kind of a dog is he?*
  - **A:** ***He's** a Border Collie. **He's very sweet** and **loves everybody…***

CD 1 ◀))) Tracks 3–6
L. LISTENING Key words. Listen again to the students in Activity C and write down the key words you hear in each introduction.

Zahid _____

_____

_____

_____

Mariana _____

_____

_____

_____

Li Ming _____

_____

_____

_____

Chul-Soo _____

_____

_____

_____

CD 1 Track 7 **M.** LISTENING Professor M. Listen to students talk about Professor M. Write down (1) the phrases used to state opinions, and (2) all the key words that give you some information about him.

PHRASES TO STATE OPINIONS	KEY WORDS TO DESCRIBE PROFESSOR M

COMMUNICATIVE STRATEGIES: *How to Talk About People*

Erika: So what's your American Lit teacher like?

Kate: Well … let's see … what do you want to know?

Erika: Everything. I think I have him next semester.

Kate: OK. **He's tall**, maybe **a little stocky**; **he has gray hair** and a gray … almost white **beard**. **He wears glasses**. **He's not** very formal, but he almost always **wears** a tie. And his shirt sleeves are always rolled up. **He wears a watch**, an old-fashioned one, not a digital one.

Erika: But what's he like as a person?

Kate: **He loves** American literature. **He's** very **patient** when we ask dumb questions. I think **he's a little bit serious,** but **he's very nice**. He just **doesn't laugh** a lot. **He seems** to really care about students**. I believe** he's a very **good teacher**. **In my opinion**, you'll like him a lot.

PHRASES

Describing People

He / She is (not) + *physical description* (tall, short, stocky, thin, bald, etc.)

He / She has + *physical description* (gray hair, blue eyes, a beard, long hair, etc.)

He / She wears + *clothing/accessories* (glasses, jewelry, jeans, t-shirts, etc.)

He / She is (is not) + *character description* (nice, considerate, patient, funny, etc.)

He / She has (doesn't have) + *character description* (a good sense of humor, patience, etc.)

He / She likes / dislikes / hates / loves / etc. + *interests* (music, movies, sports, camping, etc.)

Asking for and Stating Opinions

What do you think about …?

How do you feel about …?

What's your opinion about …"

I think …

I believe …

I'm convinced …

It seems to me that …

Note: See the *Speaker's Handbook* on page 165 for additional phrases.

N. Opinions. In each short description, replace the <u>underlined</u> word(s) with one or more opposites.

> **Example:** He's **thin**.
> He's <u>big (stocky, heavy, overweight, etc.).</u>

1. She's **young**. _____

2. She's **not good looking**. _____

3. He's **short**. _____

4. He has **long** hair. _____

5. He's **clean shaven**. _____

6. She wears **ugly** clothes. _____

7. He's a very **interesting** person. _____

8. She's a **mean** person. _____

9. She **loves** classical music. _____

10. He's **lazy**. _____

Professional Context: Talking about People

Gossip and personal criticism in professional settings is considered unprofessional in almost all circumstances. It is risky to talk about colleagues to other people you work with, because those people might not agree with or even be offended by what you're saying. There is also the chance that the person you're bad-mouthing will find out about your comments. Such actions in the workplace can make people lose trust in you professionally and personally. It's best to keep your opinions about your coworkers to yourself and to focus on positive aspects of your work situation. As in most areas of life, if you have nothing nice to say about someone, it's better to say nothing.

O. Opinion or fact? Write an **O** next to the statements you think are opinions and an **F** next to the statements you think are facts. Then write the word or phrase that made you decide one way or the other.

1. _____ He never listens to jazz. _____

2. _____ I think maybe she's still in Europe. _____

3. _____ It seems to me he should study harder. _____

4. _____ I can't believe they would just ignore you. _____

5. _____ She told me she had the flu last weekend. _____

6. _____ It's my view that they don't care about the environment. _____

7. _____ The teacher gave him a C on his essay. _____

8. _____ I really think she's ambitious. _____

9. _____ He's going back to Pakistan this summer. _____

10. _____ I thought the party was kind of boring. _____

P. A friend is someone who … Write down descriptive words to give a definition of what you think a friend is. You can use single adjectives (e.g., smart, funny) or sentence fragments (e.g., a person who accepts me for who I am, who doesn't criticize me). Then write down a couple of phrases to state your opinions. Use phrases from the **Communicative Strategies**.

_____

_____

_____

_____

_____

TALK

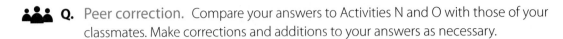

Q. Peer correction. Compare your answers to Activities N and O with those of your classmates. Make corrections and additions to your answers as necessary.

R. A friend is someone who … With your classmates, discuss your opinions of what a friend is. Use your ideas and phrases from Activity P. Those who are listening can react by agreeing or disagreeing, stating their opinions, asking for clarification, additional information, and examples.

Language Focus: Talking on the Phone

Phone conversations are different from face-to-face conversations because spoken words are not supported by visual clues such as gestures. Many non-native speakers of a language feel very anxious when they have to call someone on the phone. It helps if you learn a few phrases to start a phone conversation. After that, the rest of the conversation is easier.

Formal calls

Hello. (Good morning. / Good afternoon. / Good evening.)
This is *(your name)* speaking.
I wonder if I could speak to someone who / *(name of specific person)*.
I would like to speak to someone who / *(name of specific person)*.
Would it be possible for me to speak to someone who / *(name of specific person)*?
I'm looking for a person who (is in charge of) / *(name of specific person)*.
I'm calling to / because …

Calls to friends

Hi, this is Kevin. Is Samantha home / there? (Could / May I speak to Samantha?)
Hey, *(person's name)*. What's up? (What's happening? / How's it going? *etc.*)
Do you have time to talk? / Is this a good time?
Am I interrupting dinner / anything important?
I'm calling because …

S. Catching up. You haven't seen your friend since the end of the school year and you're calling to catch up with him or her. Use appropriate phrases to start the conversation and then tell your friend about someone you recently met. If you both have cell phones, you can stand in different parts of the room and use the phones. If not, you can turn your back on your classmate so that you don't see each other.

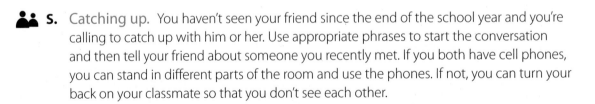

IMPROVISE

CD 1
Tracks
8–9

T. LISTENING Phone conversations. Talk about what's going on in the phone conversations you hear (the main topics and details). Then give your opinion about what the people said and discuss what they could have said or done differently.

Example: *If I were in his shoes, I would have …*

U. Ask me about … On a piece of paper, write down three topics that you would like your classmates to ask you about. Then move around the room and start conversations with different people as you show them your topics. They'll ask you questions. Use phrases from the **Communicative Strategies**.

V. A person who influenced me. Talk to a classmate about a person in your life who has influenced you a great deal. Describe the person and his or her relationship to you. Explain how he or she influenced the kind of person you are today and the choices you've made in your life. Use phrases from the **Communicative Strategies**.

W. Party conversations. Pretend that you and your classmates are at a party. Go to one person and start a conversation with him or her. The rule is that you have to keep the conversation going until your instructor tells you that you can move on to the next person. Use the phrases from the **Communicative Strategies** to start the conversations and to keep them going.

INTERNET RESEARCH Portraits of the famous. Visit websites of different people you'd like to know more about. Some examples might include entertainers, sports figures, politicians, writers, scientists, explorers, actors, movie directors, etc. After you've read a few descriptions, choose one that you find particularly interesting and tell your classmates about the person. Give as many details as possible.

1 At the Museum

"What do you think about this painting?"

Strategies for Communication

Part 1: How to React to an Image

Part 2: How to Tell a Story

👀 PREPARE 👀

A. PRE-LISTENING A variety of images. For each image, complete the information indicated.

Photograph of a town in Germany

Example:

General Subject: Street scene in a town in Germany

Key Words: houses, blue sky, shops (stores), people (shoppers), umbrellas, awnings, street vendors

Dominant Colors: shades of red, yellows, brown, black, blue, splashes of green

Like / Dislike: _____ Like _____

Painting by Vincent Van Gogh, 1890

1. General Subject: _____

Key Words: _____

Dominant Colors: _____

Like / Dislike: _____

Graffiti in Copenhagen, Denmark

2. General Subject: _____

Key Words: _____

Dominant Colors: _____

Like / Dislike: _____

Painting by Maurice Brazil
Prendergast, 1916–1918

3. General Subject: _____

Key Words: _____

Dominant Colors: _____

Like / Dislike: _____

Photograph: Hurricane Irene,
August 26, 2011

4. General Subject: _____

Key Words: _____

Dominant Colors: _____

Like / Dislike: _____

Photograph: Tripolis, 1958

5. General Subject: _____

Key Words: _____

Dominant Colors: _____

Like / Dislike: _____

B. LISTENING **Preferences.** For each of the short conversations decide whether the person likes, dislikes, or doesn't understand the piece of art being discussed.

	LIKE	DISLIKE	DOESN'T UNDERSTAND
1.			
2.			
3.			
4.			
5.			
6.			

CD 1
Track 16

C. LISTENING **Special exhibit: Laurence Young.** Look at the two paintings from the Laurence Young exhibit as you listen to the museum guide talk about them. Then answer the questions. You'll discuss these paintings with your classmates.

Pitched, **2010**   *Lattice Work*, **2010**

1. What did Young do in his childhood that continues to inspire his artwork?

_____

_____

2. What are some of the main subjects of his paintings?

_____

3. What moods is Young most interested in suggesting in his artwork?

_____

4. According to the guide, what's one of the differences between *Pitched* and *Lattice Work*?

_____

5. What words would you choose to describe *Pitched*?

_____

6. What words would you choose to describe *Lattice Work*?

_____

_____

7. Which of the two paintings do you like better? Explain.

_____

_____

_____

COMMUNICATIVE STRATEGIES: *How to React to an Image*

Alex: **What do you think about** this piece?

Carol: Hm … **I'm not sure. I'm not crazy about** abstract art.

Alex: **I prefer art that makes me think**, like this piece. **It's awesome.**

Carol: **Do you have any idea what** this is about?

Alex: Well, it's always a matter of opinion. This one **makes me think of** a city. The way you'd see it from an airplane. All the reddish, yellow and brown shapes are the roofs of houses. The green shapes are **maybe** gardens and parks. And the blue shapes might be swimming pools.

Carol: That's **interesting**. I would never have thought of that.

Paul Klee, *Mountain Village (Autumnal)*, 1934

PHRASES

Questions	Answers
What do you think about …?	I like / love / dislike / prefer …
Do you like it?	I dislike / don't like art that …
Do you have any idea what …?	doesn't depict anything.
	looks like a kid did it.
Is this the kind of art you like / prefer?	I like / love / prefer art that …
What type of art do you like?	(tells a story, has a message, makes me think, makes me dream, makes me ask questions, is simple, is colorful, depicts real life, says something, *etc.*)
What's your impression of …?	My favorite type of art is …
Why do you like / dislike / prefer …?	I'm (not) crazy about …
	It doesn't do anything for me.
Which …do you like / prefer?	I'm not sure I have a favorite. / … what to think. / … what to say.
	I don't know much about art, but …
What do you like about …?	I can't figure it out. / I don't understand it. / I don't get it. / I have no idea what it's about.
How do you feel about …?	
What do you think this painting / piece is about?	The subject / scene is …
	It reminds me of …
What do you think the artist is trying to say?	It makes me think of …
	It seems / Maybe …
	It symbolizes / suggests …

Descriptive Adjectives to Express Opinions

Positive: amazing / awesome / beautiful / cool / extraordinary / fabulous / fantastic / gorgeous / impressive / incredible / interesting / lovely / remarkable / terrific / unique / wonderful

Less Positive / Negative: awful / bizarre / bland / boring / horrible / mediocre / nice / not bad / OK / ordinary / strange / ugly

Note: See the *Speaker's Handbook* on page 165 for additional phrases.

D. What do you think about this one? For each question, first write a general statement and then give a reason. Use phrases and adjectives from the **Communicative Strategies**.

Example: What do you think about this one?

It doesn't do anything for me. I'm not crazy about abstract art.

OR

It's OK. I prefer art that says something.

1. What about this one?

_____

2. Is this the kind of art you like?

_____

3. What's your impression of this painting?

_____

4. How do you feel about this artist?

_____

5. What do you like about this painting?

_____

6. Do you like abstract art?

_____

7. Which of Laurence Young's paintings do you prefer?

_____

8. What do you think this piece is about?

_____

Language Focus: Types of Painting

When you describe something you saw and the person you're talking to isn't actually looking at the piece, it's easiest to start with the type of painting and the subject. The following are some of the basic types of painting you can use.

*It's an **abstract*** work of art with lots of geometric shapes.

*It's a **landscape*** of a lake in the mountains.

*It's a **portrait*** of a young boy.

*It's a **still life*** (plural = ***still lifes***) of fruits and vegetables.

*It's a **seascape*** of a kayak race on the ocean.

*It's a **real life / representational*** painting of people working in a factory.

*It's a **historical*** piece that depicts a Native American village.

Other types of visual arts: photographs / sculptures / drawings / sketches / posters / pottery / ceramics / fashion design / graphic arts / graffiti / tattoos (body art) / cartoons / architecture / films / prints / murals (wall art) / carpentry (furniture) / totem poles / blankets / wood carvings

E. What I want to say. First, write down phrases and words from the **Communicative Strategies** and the **Language Focus** that you want to use to describe the types of images you prefer. Then, write down the reasons for your preferences.

F. Special exhibit: Marcia Dalbey. For each of the two paintings by Marcia Dalbey, write down (1) the types of paintings and general subjects, (2) key words about the content, and (3) your reactions to the pieces and the reasons for them. You'll be talking with your classmates about the two paintings, so make as many notes about them as possible.

Marcia Dalbey, *Market Day,* **2007**

1. _____

_____

_____

_____

_____

_____

_____

Marcia Dalbey, *Waiting,* **2008**

2. _____

_____

_____

_____

_____

_____

_____

Professional Context: Art Is Big Business

In the past, the buying and selling of art was reserved for wealthy collectors who wanted to show off their artwork in their homes. Once they obtained a certain piece, they often held on to it for generations. Today, the situation is very different. Art has become very big business with millions of dollars worth of art sold and bought as investments. Those who can afford to buy a Picasso when it comes up for auction, for example, might hold on to it just long enough to be able to resell it at a big profit. Some people collect art of newer artists in the hope that these artists will become famous in the future. At that point, these collectors can then resell the art for much more than they originally paid for it.

TALK

G. Peer correction. With your classmates, compare your answers to Activity D. Make corrections and additions to your answers as necessary.

H. My favorite types of images. Using the notes you made in Activity E, talk to your classmates about the kinds of images you like to look at and why. Your classmates can ask you questions for clarification, additional information, and examples.

I. Special exhibit: Laurence Young. Participate in the class discussion of the two paintings by Laurence Young in Activity C. Listen to what others have to say about the paintings, add your own ideas, and explain why you prefer one painting over the other (or like them both equally).

J. Paintings by Marcia Dalbey. With a group of classmates, talk about the two paintings by the artist Marcia Dalbey in Activity F. Use your notes to ask questions, give your opinions, and state your preferences. Listen carefully to what your classmates have to say so that you can ask them questions for clarification or additional information.

Part Two

LISTENING COMPREHENSION: *Sequencing Your Ideas*

When you tell a story, it's important to put your ideas in the correct order so that the events of your story are clear to your listeners. The best way to sequence ideas and events is to use phrases that establish the beginning, the middle, and the end of the story. The following is a list of some sequencing phrases.

Beginning: first, to begin with, to start (off) with, on Tuesday …,   last month …, *etc.*
Middle: then, next, after that, before that, the day before, earlier, at 10 o'clock, *etc.*
Interruptions: suddenly, all of a sudden, without warning, *etc.*
Simultaneous events: while, as, at the same time, *etc.*
Ending: eventually, in the end, finally, the whole thing ended with …, *etc.*

CD 1 🔊
Track 17

K. LISTENING What happened when? Listen to the conversation between Diane and her husband Tony. As you listen, number the events in the order they took place. Then, to the right of the sentence, write the word or expression that's used to sequence the event, if one is used.

_____ School called. _____

_____ Drove the kids to school. _____

_____ Nancy sent a text about the cat. _____

_____ Husband left the house and everything fell apart. _____

_____ Put in a load of laundry. _____

_____ Husband put dinner in the oven. _____

_____ Mom brought permission slip to school. _____

_____ Called mom to pick up kids from school. _____

_____ Called mom again to ask her to bring permission slip to school. _____

_____ Husband got home and started the washing machine. _____

_____ Organizing kids and boss called. _____

_____ Clients called. _____

_____ Went to work. _____

_____ Nancy took cat to the vet. _____

_____ Ate an energy bar. _____

_____ Stopped the washing machine. _____

L. LISTENING A fender bender. Listen to the conversation and (1) write down the words that have to do with the car accident, and (2) write down the words that sequence the events.

WORDS ASSOCIATED WITH THE CAR ACCIDENT	WORDS / PHRASES TO SEQUENCE EVENTS

COMMUNICATIVE STRATEGIES: *How to Tell a Story*

Tim: I took this picture **the day after** Hurricane Irene went up the East Coast. It was at **the end of August, in 2011.**

Abby: So where is this?

Tim: It's one of the streets in New York City.

Abby: From what I saw on TV, the storm must have been really frightening.

Tim: It was the worst I'd ever been in. When it **first** came up the coast, we weren't too worried. But **then** the weather reports got worse and worse. And, when it **eventually** got to us, we were terrified. It's like it came **out of nowhere**. The amount of rain was unbelievable. The wind was crazy. **Before** the storm, a lot of people went to shelters. We lost electricity almost **right away. Picture it**, most of the East Coast without power. **Finally, after** it was all over, it took forever to clean up the mess.

PHRASES

(So) Here's what happened.

Picture this / it.

So here's the story.

There's a whole story behind this.

You'll never believe this / what happened!

I can't believe this happened (to me).

The story / movie / painting / book is about …

To begin with … / First (of all) … / To start with …

Then, … / Next, … / (Right) After that, …

Finally, … / In the end, … / Eventually, … / It all ended with …

At the same time that / While / As …

Suddenly, … / (Then) Out of nowhere …

As soon as …

Right away, … / Immediately …

In addition, …

Therefore, … / As a result, …

Time indicators: last year / two years ago / last month / two weeks ago / at ten thirty / yesterday (morning, afternoon, evening) / last night / during (the party, dinner, etc.) / today / tomorrow (morning, afternoon, evening) / this (morning, afternoon, evening) / the day before yesterday / the next day / the following day / the day after / June 5th, 2011

Note: See the *Speaker's Handbook* on page 165 for additional phrases.

M. Story fragments. Complete each story fragment logically with words or phrases from the **Communicative Strategies**.

Example: _____ When I got to his house, he was in a total

panic. His dog had just run away. _Here's what happened._____   OR

_You'll never believe this._____ etc.

1. And then he told me he was leaving me.

That really came _____. _____ he also

decided he wanted all the furniture and the car.

2. _____ we got to the cabin, we _____

unpacked all our stuff. _____ we went swimming in the lake.

_____ we were swimming, Dad got the barbecue ready.

3. _____ it rained all day. _____

we decided to go to the museum. We walked around the Egyptian exhibit.

_____ we went and had a great lunch at the museum

restaurant. _____ we went to the store and bought a present

for Grandma's birthday. _____ we went home and watched a

game on TV.

4. _____ we went on a two-week trip to Costa Rica.

We left from Miami on _____ and flew into San José.

_____ two nights in San José, we started our bus tour.

_____ we visited a coffee plantation. _____

we visited a local school. _____ we went kayaking on Lake

Arenal. _____ we explored a couple of national parks and a

tropical forest. _____ we went back to San José and flew back

to the U.S.

5. I didn't get any sleep _____. _____.

I was home alone when I _____ heard a noise at the

back door. I rushed to see what was going on and I saw that the doorknob was

turning very slowly. _____ I completely freaked out.

_____ I grabbed my baseball bat and started yelling. The knob

stopped turning. When I _____ calmed down, I heard Dad's

voice telling me to calm down. But, _____ I was so stressed

out that I couldn't sleep.

Language Focus: Using the Present Tense to Tell Stories

When you tell a personal story, you usually talk about something that happened in the past and you therefore use past tenses.

> Here's what **happened**. I **was driving** along Route 28. There **was** a lot of traffic and we **were going** pretty slowly.

However, it's just as likely that you use the present tense if you want the person to imagine exactly how the events occurred.

> So **picture** this. I'**m driving** along Route 28. There'**s** a lot of traffic and we'**re going** pretty slowly.

The present tense is also generally used when you tell the story (plot) of a movie or a book or when you talk about the story in a work of art.

> The movie (book) **is** about three friends who **decide** to rob a bank. They **plan** every detail of the heist. But one of the guys **tells** his girlfriend all about it. …

> In these three paintings, the artist **is giving** us a scene from his childhood. Here he'**s exploring** the woods. In this one, he **sits** in school, looking out of the window at the birds. And here he'**s sitting** on the beach.

N. A fairy tale. On a separate piece of paper, make a basic outline of the plot of a fairy tale you heard or read. To sequence the events properly, include words and phrases from the **Communicative Strategies**. You'll be telling your story to one of your classmates.

Cultural Connections: Children's Stories

In the United States, as in most cultures, children grow up with fairy tales and simple children's stories. These stories are intended to introduce young kids to books, reading, and the world of imagination. Classic fairy tales like *Little Red Riding Hood*, *Cinderella*, *Sleeping Beauty*, and *The Princess and the Frog*, usually start with the phrase "Once upon a time, …" and, in the American versions, always have a happy ending. As adults, most of us remember these stories very well.

What stories and tales do you remember from your childhood? How did you first hear them? Why do you think you remember them?

●● TALK ●●

O. **Peer correction.** With your classmates, compare your answers to Activity M. Make corrections and additions to your answers as necessary.

P. **A fairy tale.** Tell your classmate the fairy tale or story that you prepared in Activity N. Your classmate can ask you questions for clarification or additional information. Use words and phrases from the **Communicative Strategies**.

Q. **What happened?** With your classmates, unscramble the images to invent the details about what happened in this car accident. Make sure that your story is sequenced logically. Use words and phrases from the **Communicative Strategies** to tell the story.

R. **A crazy day!** Tell your classmates about a crazy day you had recently. Give all the details and make sure to sequence the events so that they make sense. Use words and phrases from the **Communicative Strategies**.

IMPROVISE

CD 1
Track 19 **S.** LISTENING Special exhibit: Two other works by Laurence Young. Look at the two paintings as the museum guide talks about them. Then, use the statements and questions provided to discuss the paintings with your classmates.

1. Describe the two paintings. Use some of the descriptions given by the guide as well as your own words.

2. Which of the two paintings do you like better? Explain. Does it bring up memories of something for you?

3. Of the four paintings by Laurence Young (here and in Activity C), which one is your favorite? Explain.

Laurence Young, *Sway*, **2010**

Laurence Young, *In Season*, **2010**

 T. Young and Dalbey. Look again at the two boats by Young and Dalbey that you saw earlier in the chapter (Activities C and F). With your classmates, compare and contrast the two paintings. Think about the titles, the details of the scene, the details of the boats, the foreground, the background, the colors and shapes, and the possible messages.

Laurence Young, *Pitched*, **2010**

Marcia Dalbey, *Waiting*, **2008**

 U. One of my favorite movies (books). Tell your classmate about a movie or book you really like. You need to tell the whole plot, or storyline, so get your classmate's permission to do so. Be as detailed as you can about the various aspects of the movie or book, and give concrete reasons why you like it so much. Use phrases from the **Communicative Strategies** to tell your story.

V. My favorite place. Describe your favorite place to your classmate. It could be something as large as a town or city or something smaller such as your room. The goal of this activity is for you to provide as detailed a description as possible. You should also include in your story when you were first in this place and how it became important to you. Use phrases from the **Communicative Strategies** for your description and for telling the story of the place.

INTERNET RESEARCH Search the Internet to find an artist who is from the same place that you are from. Read about this person so that you can talk to your classmates about his or her life and artwork. If you want to, you can print samples of the artwork by this person and bring them to class so that your classmates can see what you're talking about.

2 Moving to a New Place

"You can help load the truck."

Strategies for Communication

Part 1: How to Give Instructions and Advice

Part 2: How to Agree and Disagree

How to Describe Places

 PREPARE

A. PRE-LISTENING Moving checklist. Write the letters of the words in the right column that match the verbs on the left to make logical phrases.

1. make _____   **a.** family and friends

2. decide _____   **b.** a truck

3. organize _____   **c.** the boxes

4. order and buy _____   **d.** what you don't want to keep

5. call _____   **e.** the utilities and the phone

6. clean out _____   **f.** your belongings

7. cancel _____   **g.** a checklist of things to do

8. file _____   **h.** your clothes

9. rent _____   **i.** the dishes

10. sort _____   **j.** the move

11. sell or give away _____   **k.** the refrigerator

12. wrap _____   **l.** your friends for help

13. pack _____   **m.** the truck and the car

14. ask _____   **n.** the date of the move

15. label and number _____   **o.** a change of address with the post office

16. load _____   **p.** cardboard boxes and tape

CD 1 🔊 Tracks 20–27   **B.** LISTENING Instructions or advice? For each of the short exchanges, decide if the person is giving instructions or advice. Put a check (✓) in the correct column.

	INSTRUCTIONS	ADVICE
1.		
2.		
3.		
4.		
5.		
6.		
7.		
8.		

CD 1 Track 28 **C.** LISTENING **What a mess!** It's the week before four friends are supposed to move out of their apartment, and there's still a lot to do. Listen to the conversation and write down the tasks each person is assigned to do.

1. Ernesto

_____

_____

2. Mike

_____

_____

3. Park

_____

_____

4. Simon

_____

_____

Sacha: While you guys are packing, why don't I go get dinner? **What do you want?**

Karen: **Why don't you** just get pizza? That's really easy.

Helen: I'm sick of pizza. I'd rather have a hamburger. Just **go** to the place next door.

Sacha: I have an idea. **Why not** go Mexican this time? I feel like eating some tacos.

Helen: Great idea. **Would you please** pick up some burritos for me? You know what I like.

Karen: **Get** me a couple of fish tacos. And **buy** plenty of chips and salsa.

PHRASES

Offering to Help
What do you want me to do?
What can I do (to help)?
What do I do next?
Tell me what to do.
What else can / should / could I do?
Where do you want me to start?

Giving Instructions
I'd like you to …
Why don't you … ?
It would really help if you could …
You can help by …
I could use help with …
Would / Could you please … ?
You could / can start by …
I need you to …
You get to …

First, you …
Next, you
After that, you …
When you're done with that, you can / could / should …
Finally, you … / The last thing you …

Note: *You can use the command form of various verbs:* go, pick up, clean, buy, *etc.*

Giving Advice
If I were you, I would(n't) …
I think you should … / I don't think you should …
(Maybe) You could …
Why not … ?
What I would do is …
Why don't you … ?

Note: See the *Speaker's Handbook* on page 165 for additional phrases.

D. **Offers of help.** Write an appropriate question or statement for each answer. In some instances, the answer is advice, while in others it's instructions. Use phrases from the **Communicative Strategies** and questions / statements you already know for asking for advice.

Examples: I don't know if I should rent a one-bedroom or a two-bedroom apartment.

If I were you, I would rent a two-bedroom apartment.

What do you want me to do?

It would really help if you could fix breakfast for the kids.

1. _____

Maybe you should finish writing your essay tonight.

2. _____

Lucky you. You get to clean the bathroom!

3. _____

Why don't you find another place to live?

4. _____

I think you should go to the doctor.

5. _____

Don't forget to get gas.

6. _____

The last thing you have to do is order the cardboard boxes.

7. _____

What I would do is get a part-time job.

8. _____

Could you please help me with the dishes?

E. **What do you want me to do?** Write a follow-up to each statement or question using the cue in parentheses and a phrase for either instructions or advice. Add an additional piece of information that you invent. Use phrases from the **Communicative Strategies**.

Example: Hey, John. We're out of milk. (pick some up)

Would you please pick some up on the way home from work?

1. I'd like to do some volunteer work, but I don't know what to do. (tutor kids)

_____

2. Hey, Suzie. It's Mom's birthday on Saturday. (order the cake)

_____

3. Come here kids. The yard is a mess. (rake the leaves)

_____

4. I don't know what classes to take next semester. (talk to advisor)

_____

5. Time for bed. (get into pajamas and brush teeth)

_____

6. Patrick is not doing well in his math class. (talk to teacher)

_____

7. I'd like to get a pet. (get two cats)

_____

8. We'd like to do something interesting for our vacation, but what? (go on a trip up the Amazon)

_____

9. What can I do to help? (pack the books)

_____

10. Eric's not here right now. (have him call me)

_____

F. **I need help with this.** Select a project (e.g., cleaning a house, planning a party, starting a club, organizing a fundraiser for a good cause, helping someone in the community, collecting food for the needy, and so on) in which you're going to involve a few of your classmates. Make a list of all the things that have to be done and select some phrases from the **Communicative Strategies** that you can use to give the others instructions.

_____

_____

_____

_____

_____

_____

_____

Professional Context: Getting Transferred to a New Place

In the United States, it's common for companies to transfer important employees to other parts of the country or even other parts of the world. In fact, some employees look for opportunities to move to places that interest them. When such possibilities come up, they may move their entire family to the new location and buy or rent a new home. When they arrive, they have to go "house hunting" so that they can find a suitable place for the whole family. These types of job transfers, or relocations, are often major moves that involve new schools for the kids, learning a new language and new customs, and adjusting to different living conditions.

TALK

G. Peer correction. With your classmates, compare your answers to Activities D and E. Make corrections and/or additions to your answers as necessary.

H. I need help with this. Explain to your classmates the project you came up with in Activity F. First, let them know that you need help. When they agree, give them instructions for what each will do. They can ask for clarification or additional information. Once you're done, another group member will talk about a project.

I. We're moving! You and your housemates are moving to another apartment. Talk about everything that has to be done, make a list, decide who will organize the move, and then assign the various tasks to everyone in the group.

J. What do you think I should do? Move around the room and give advice and instructions about **one** of the following problems each classmate presents to you. As you give advice and instructions, you'll be asked for clarification and additional information. When you're done with one problem, reverse roles. Then, move on to another classmate.

Example: Your classmate wants to visit family in Canada. But he / she is afraid of flying.
> **Your classmate:** *I want to visit my family in Canada, but I'm afraid of flying.*
> **You:** *Well, you could take the bus.*
> **Your classmate:** *I wouldn't know how to do that.*
> **You:** *It's really simple. First, you go online and look at the bus schedules. Then, you find out how to buy the ticket. If I were you, I would travel during the weekend ...*
> **Your classmate:** *Won't the trip take forever?...*

Problems

1. Your classmate's cousin is getting married. He / She has been invited to the wedding, but the event is during the same week as final exams. What could / should your classmate do?

2. Your classmate's neighbor asked him / her to babysit three kids. He / She feels obligated to do it but doesn't know what to do.

3. Your classmate's dog got out of the house. He / She asks you what to do and how to organize a search party.

4. Your classmate wants to join a gym but it's much too expensive. What can he / she do to get exercise without spending a lot of money?

5. Your classmate wants to organize a surprise party for your English instructor. But he / she can't figure out everything that has to be done.

Part Two

●● PREPARE ●●

LISTENING COMPREHENSION: *Spatial Relationships and Directional Words*

Organizing the furniture in a room, navigating around a city, or telling someone how to find something are all situations that require words that describe locations, spatial relationships, and directions. How accurately you follow directions and instructions depends on how well you understand these words when you hear them.

Location: *in* (in enclosed spaces, in places with borders, in bodies of water), *on* (on the surface), *at* (at a place)

Spatial relationships: *above (over, on top of), across (from), opposite, against, ahead of (in front of), among, around, behind (in back of), below (under / underneath, beneath), beside, between, far (from), in, near, next to, through, toward*

Language Focus: Using *in* and *on* with Modes of Transportation

In general,
- *in* is used with a car: *I left the keys **in** the car (taxi, cab, limo).*
- *on* is used with public or commercial means of transportation:
  *The people **on** the bus (subway / plane / bus / train / boat) were scared.*
  *She left her bag **on** the bus (subway / plane / bus / train / boat).*
- *on* can also be used with two-wheeled modes of transportation:
  *I went there **on** my bike. (I took my bike.)*
  *He came **on** his motorcycle. (He used his motorcycle.)*

Directional words:
- *–ward (backward, forward, sideward, upward, downward, northward, etc.)*
- compass points: *north, south, east, west, northeast (northwest), southeast (southwest)*

Additional words of location: *inside, outside, upstairs, downstairs, on the first / second (etc.) floor, up, down, in front of, in back of, at the front, at the back, toward, into, right here / there, over here / there, in the same place as*

CD 1 Tracks 29–38 **K.** LISTENING Where? Listen to each dialogue, and write down the phrase that's used to indicate the location in the appropriate column in the chart. A dialogue may have more than one answer.

	AT A SPECIFIC PLACE	IN AN ENCLOSED SPACE, A PLACE WITH BORDERS, OR A BODY OF WATER	ON A SURFACE
1.			
2.			
3.			
4.			
5.			
6.			
7.			
8.			
9.			
10.			

CD 1 🔊
Track 39

L. **LISTENING** **Moving into a new place.** Listen to the conversation between Sarah and Jamal as they unpack their belongings in their new home. Then, mark each statement as true (T) or false (F). Correct the false statements.

Janie, Jamal, Sarah, and Alyssa   Percy   Unpacking the clothes

1. _____ The girls and Percy are running around while the parents are unpacking.

_____

2. _____ Jamal is the one who is organizing the unpacking.

_____

3. _____ Jamal disagrees with Sarah about starting with the kitchen.

_____

4. _____ They end up agreeing and setting up the kitchen first.

_____

5. _____ After the kids' room, they plan to set up their own bedroom.

_____

6. _____ The reason for unpacking the clothes is to get rid of the boxes in the living room.

_____

7. _____ Janie and Alyssa have separate bedrooms.

_____

8. _____ Their new house is near a park, a school, a grocery store, and work.

_____

9. _____ They're not going to get a second cat.

_____

10. _____ Jamal was nervous about the move, but now he thinks that change is good.

_____

COMMUNICATIVE STRATEGIES: *How to Agree and Disagree / How to Describe Places*

Lori: I know you disagree with me, **but I really don't think** we should buy this house.

Carl: Look, **it's** the right **price**, **it's** the perfect **size**, **it has** a great **yard**, **it's on a quiet street**, and **it's close** to work.

Lori: **All of that's true, but you have to admit** that the place is a mess. Every room has to be repainted …

Carl: **You're right**, but that's not a big deal. We can do it ourselves.

Lori: **Agreed. But** what about all the plumbing problems?

Carl: **I'll give you that one.** We'll have to hire a plumber.

Lori: **Now you're making sense. But** that'll be very expensive. And the windows are in miserable shape, and the whole master bathroom has to be redone.

Carl: **I'll grant you that**. Yes, it'll take some money. But we can bring in someone to replace the windows and I'll redo the bathroom.

Lori: **Are you serious?** When are you planning to do all that? Before you go to work at six or after you get home at eight for a late dinner?

Carl: Hm … **I hadn't thought of that**. The house is very interesting but **I can see your point. It has** too many **problems**. Let's keep looking.

PHRASES

Agreeing

All of that's true, but …
(Yes / OK) You're right (about that).
Agreed. / I agree.
I'll give you that. / I'll grant you that (one).
(Now) you're making sense.

I hadn't thought of that.
I can see your point.
That's a good point.
OK. Why not?
Sounds good / logical / about right.
Good idea!

Disagreeing

But …
(But) You have to admit …
Are you serious? / You can't be serious!
I (really) don't think …
You can't possibly think that!

That doesn't make any sense.
That's insane! / ridiculous! / nuts!
That's not a good idea.
I'd rather … / Instead …
I'm not sure …
I disagree.
What are you thinking!

Describing Places

It's / It looks + *adjective* (interesting / perfect / beautiful)

It's + *directional words* (in / at / on / far from / near / behind / across from)

It's + *noun* (a mess / a fixer-upper / an antique / a walk-in closet)

It has + *noun* (a great yard / character / lot's of space / a pool / a patio)

Note: See the *Speaker's Handbook* on page 165 for additional phrases.

M. I disagree. Disagree with each statement. Use a phrase from the **Communicative Strategies** and give a reason for your disagreement.

Example: I think we should stay at home this summer.

You can't be serious! We haven't had a vacation in almost a year.

I need to get away from here.

1. I'm sick of our old furniture. Let's go buy some new things.

_____

2. I'm going to repaint the living room red.

_____

3. He thinks he wants to move to Alaska.

_____

4. Instead of going to college, she's thinking of going into the military.

_____

5. I'm going to do the electrical wiring myself.

_____

6. In my opinion, we should bring in a landscaper to redo our front yard.

_____

7. I'm going to invite the whole neighborhood to the party.

_____

8. I vote for buying the house on River Drive. It's perfect for us.

_____

Cultural Connections: House Hunting

The idea of "house hunting" is so popular in the United States that there are even TV programs about people looking at homes in the United States and internationally. People who are "house hunting" might want to rent or buy an apartment or house. They usually go to a real estate agency, they describe what they're looking for and how much they can afford to pay, and then they look at several places that might suit them. Since choosing a new home is usually a very important decision in people's lives, the "house hunting" process can take quite a bit of time.

How do people find a new home where you're from? When young people get married, how do they find a home to rent or to buy? How do they make the decision to live in a particular place?

N. Our new house. For each statement, first agree with what is being said and then give a description as a reason for your agreement. Use phrases from the **Communicative Strategies**.

Example: This house is big enough for the five of us.

You're right. It has 4 bedrooms, one for us and one for each of the kids.

1. I think we'd better hire an electrician to rewire the heating system.

_____

2. Maybe we should convert this room into an office.

_____

3. What if we repainted the kitchen a light shade of yellow?

_____

4. I'm going to plant some fruit trees in the backyard.

_____

5. Don't you think that the couch would look better over here?

_____

6. I think tomorrow we should take a long walk around the neighborhood.

_____

7. These door locks are a real problem. None of them work.

_____

8. We don't have enough money to make all the repairs.

_____

O. My dream house. Imagine that you're going to go house hunting. Make some descriptive notes about where you want the house to be located, what you want it to be like, in what kind of neighborhood, etc. Then, write a reason for five of the descriptive details. Use phrases from the **Communicative Strategies**.

Example: *I want a place in New York City. It's the most interesting city in the United States.*

_____

_____

_____

_____

_____

_____

_____

TALK

P. Peer correction. With your classmates, compare your answers to Activities M and N. Make corrections and/or additions to your answers as necessary.

Q. My dream house. Talk to your classmate about the dream house you described in Activity N. Say where it's located, give a detailed description of the neighborhood and the house, and give reasons for your choice. Your classmate will either agree or disagree with your reasons. When you're done, reverse roles.

Example: **You:** *I want a place in New York City. It's the most interesting city in the United States.*
Your classmate: *I guess New York is OK. But I disagree with you. I don't think it's the most interesting city. I've been there and I really prefer San Francisco.*
OR
I agree with you. There's no place like New York City.

R. Where I grew up. Give your classmates a detailed description of where you grew up. Talk about the location, the neighborhood, your house. Say what you liked and what you didn't like about it. Your classmates can ask questions for clarification and additional information. Use phrases from the **Communicative Strategies**.

S. Problems, problems. You and your classmates talk about the problems listed. One of you brings up the problem. The others ask questions, give opinions about what to do, and all of you agree or disagree with the solutions proposed.

1. My kids refuse to eat fruit and vegetables. All they're interested in is stuff like pizza, spaghetti, and hamburgers. I don't know what to do to get them to eat some healthier foods.
2. I really want to do some volunteer work so that I can help the less fortunate people in my community. But I have no idea what to do or how to get started.
3. I saw a student cheat on a test in my psychology class. I have no idea what to do about it.
4. I need to get a job, but I have no idea how I can possibly combine school with work. Should I just quit school until I make enough money? Should I look for a job that will still leave me time to take some classes?
5. It's taking me at least an hour to get to school every day because I have to take three different buses. Then, it takes me at least another hour to get back to my apartment. That's a lot of commuting. Something has to change.

T. Do you agree? You and your classmates discuss the issues listed below. State your opinions, give examples, ask questions, agree, and disagree. Use phrases from the **Communicative Strategies**.

Issues:

1. People should be willing to give up some things so that they spend less and waste less.
2. People should be willing to do their part to make the world a cleaner place.
3. Everyone should do everything possible to help at least one person in the community.
4. Social media have become the most important communication tool in today's world.
5. Everyone should do things to have a more healthy physical, intellectual, and emotional life.
6. One of the main goals in life is to own your own house.

IMPROVISE

U. LISTENING We agree … this is the house for us. Listen to the conversation between Lori and Carl as they continue to look for a new house. Then use the questions that follow to have a discussion with your classmates.

The first house:

1. What are Lori's objections to the house?

2. What two answers does Carl have to counter Lori's objections?

3. What argument finally convinces Carl that Lori is right?

The second house:

4. What objections does Lori have to the house? Are they serious objections?

5. Based on the images and Lori's and Carl's descriptions, what's the house like?

6. Why is this house perfect for entertaining?

7. What does Carl say at the end to be even more convincing?

V. Let's help. You and your classmates talk about different projects you could do to help someone in your community. After you've agreed on a project and outlined the details, select one person of the group to be in charge. That person then gives instructions to the others. Everyone can ask questions, give opinions, agree, and disagree.

W. An interesting place. Describe to your classmate an interesting place you've visited or seen on TV. Give as many details as possible. Your classmate can ask questions for clarification and additional information. Use phrases from the **Communicative Strategies**.

X. **The story of a move.** You and your classmates invent a story of someone's move from one home to another. First, describe the family that's moving (including pets, if they have any). Then, talk about the date of the move, problems of packing the belongings, complications, and anything else you can add to make the story interesting. Everyone in the group has to contribute to the story. You may use the images that follow to help you with ideas for the conversation, but you do not need to base your story on the images. Use phrases from the **Communicative Strategies**.

INTERNET RESEARCH House hunting Go online and search for real estate ads to find a few houses that seem to fit the dream house and the location you described in Activity N. Tell your classmates about the houses. For each ad, say how it does or does not match the idea of your dream house.

3 Thanksgiving Dinner
"We're so glad you could join us!"

Strategies for Communication

Part 1: How to Respond to Invitations

Part 2: How to Interact Socially

Part One

●● PREPARE ●●

A. **PRE-LISTENING Thanksgiving dinner.** Read the menu for a traditional American Thanksgiving dinner. Then answer the questions.

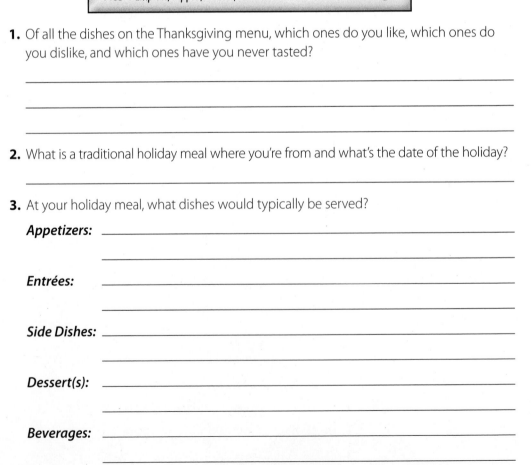

HAPPY THANKSGIVING!
November 28, 2013

Appetizers
Butternut Squash Soup
Mixed Green Salad with Apples and Walnuts

Entrée
Roast Turkey with Sausage Stuffing

Side Dishes
Mashed Potatoes and Gravy
Sweet Potatoes with Marshmallows
Green Bean Casserole
Steamed Brussels Sprouts with Walnuts
Peas, Carrots, Pearl Onions in White Sauce

Cranberry Sauce
Rolls and Herb Butter

Dessert
Pies: Pumpkin, Apple, Pecan, Custard

1. Of all the dishes on the Thanksgiving menu, which ones do you like, which ones do you dislike, and which ones have you never tasted?

_____

_____

_____

2. What is a traditional holiday meal where you're from and what's the date of the holiday?

_____

3. At your holiday meal, what dishes would typically be served?

Appetizers: _____

_____

Entrées: _____

_____

Side Dishes: _____

_____

Dessert(s): _____

_____

Beverages: _____

_____

B. **LISTENING I can't wait to eat!** Listen to the conversation between Sandra and James as they finish the preparations for their Thanksgiving dinner. Then answer the questions on a separate sheet of paper.

1. Who are Sandra and James and who have they invited for Thanksgiving dinner?
2. Who did the shopping, and who set the table and prepared the dinner?
3. What are they going to do if they have too much food?
4. Where are Yoshiro's parents originally from? How do you know?
5. What do we know about Karen and Yoshiro?
6. What's the announcement that Sandra is talking about?
7. How does James react to that idea?
8. How do you know that James has probably changed his mind by the end of the conversation and is more positive about the idea?
9. Is Karen an only child? What is said that supports your answer?
10. What do you learn about Tony?
11. What's Sandra hoping for?

CD 2
Tracks
2–4

C. **LISTENING It's nice to finally meet you!** Listen to the segments of conversation between the hosts and the guests. Then answer the questions on a separate sheet of paper.

Shiro and Hana Matsuo   *Karen O'Donnell and Yoshiro Matsuo*

Segment 1

1. What's the first thing Sandra says to the Matsuos when they arrive at the house? Why do you think she's being formal?
2. What phrases does Karen use to introduce the two sets of parents?
3. Had Yoshiro already met Karen's parents? How do you know?
4. When James says, "We've heard a lot about you," why is this a nice thing to say to the Matsuos?

Segment 2

5. What does Hana bring Sandra as a house gift and why did she choose that gift?

6. What's the polite phrase that Sandra uses when she accepts the gift? What meaning do you think that phrase really has?

7. Besides saying "Thank you," what does Sandra say to let Hana know that the gift is appreciated?

8. Of the two mothers, which one first invites the other one to use first names? Which of the two fathers first does the same?

Segment 3

9. How does Sandra encourage Shiro and Hana to talk about something they like to do?

10. What do the two couples have in common?

11. How can you tell that the four parents are starting to become friends?

COMMUNICATIVE STRATEGIES: *How to Respond to Invitations*

Sandra: Hello, Mrs. Matsuo? This is Sandra O'Donnell, Karen's mother.

Hana: Oh, hello, Mrs. O'Donnell.

Sandra: **I'm calling to invite** you and your husband to have Thanksgiving dinner with us on the 24th. With Karen and Yoshiro, of course. **We would be very pleased** if you could join us. It would give us the chance to meet.

Hana: Karen already invited us informally and she said I would be getting a call from you. My husband and I are **happy to accept** your invitation. **Thank you so much** for thinking of us. **Is there anything** we can bring?

Sandra: Not really. I have everything under control. Just bring a big appetite. There'll be lots of food.

PHRASES

Inviting
I'm calling to invite …
I'd like to invite …
Would you like to …?
How would you like to …?
Can you …?
Are you free on / to …?
What're you doing on …?
Why don't we … ?
Let's …
Do you want to / wanna …?
What would you say to …?
Wanna …?

Accepting
… happy / pleased to accept …
Thank you so much.
Thanks for thinking of me / us.
Yes, I'd / we'd love to …
Thanks for inviting me / us.
Thanks for the invitation.
I'll / We'll be there.
That'll be fun. Thanks. I'd / We'd love to come.

Saying "no" nicely
Sorry, I can't. I'm / We're …
Thanks. But …
I'm afraid I / we can't …
Sorry, I / we already have other plans.
Thanks for asking, but …
I wish I could. But I / we …
That's very nice of you. But I / we …

Note: See the *Speaker's Handbook* on page 165 for additional phrases.

You can be fairly direct in your response to an invitation with people you know well. These are some of the phrases you might use. Notice their informality.

Thanks, but I'm not in the mood to …

I feel lazy. I (don't) want to …

I just wanna hang out. (I just wanna chill.)

I don't wanna do anything.

I don't feel like it. I'd rather …

I don't know. It doesn't sound like much fun.

D. How would you like to …? Write a logical invitation for each response. Pay attention to the formality or informality of the response. Use phrases from the **Communicative Strategies**.

1. _____

   Thank you so much for inviting us. We'd be happy to join you.

2. _____

   I don't think so. I'd rather just hang out here.

3. _____

   We're pleased to accept your invitation. At what time should we be there?

4. _____

   Sorry, I can't. I'll be out of town that week.

5. _____

   You go without me. I'm not in the mood to do anything.

6. _____

   I'm afraid we can't be there. It's our son's birthday and we have plans.

7. _____

   That'll be fun. I'll definitely be there.

8. _____

   I wish I could. But I have a meeting that night.

E. You're invited. For each invitation, first write a phrase to accept and then a phrase to say "no" politely. Pay attention to the formality or informality of the invitation. Use phrases from the **Communicative Strategies** and the **Language Focus**.

1. What would you say to going camping with us? We'll be gone two days.

   Accept _____

   Say "no" _____

2. I'm calling to invite you to Thanksgiving dinner. I hope you can make it.

   Accept _____

   Say "no" _____

3. Do you wanna go to the pool?

Accept _____

Say "no" _____

4. Would you like to come over to watch the football game?

Accept _____

Say "no" _____

5. Are you free this Saturday? We're thinking of going to the beach.

Accept _____

Say "no" _____

6. Why don't we go to the concert tonight?

Accept _____

Say "no" _____

F. Do you want to …? You're going to invite different classmates to do something with you. First, make a list of the possible activities (e.g., asking someone to go have coffee after class). Then write down the phrases you want to use to make the invitation. You'll also be asked to do things, so write down phrases to accept and say "no" nicely.

When you're doing the inviting

1. List of activities

_____

_____

_____

_____

2. Phrases for making the invitations

_____

_____

When you're being invited

3. phrases to accept (formal and informal)

_____

4. phrases to say "no" politely and a reason

_____

5. phrases to say "no" with classmates you know well

_____

TALK

G. Peer correction. Compare your answers to Activities D and E with your classmates. Make corrections and/or additions to your answers as necessary.

H. Do you want to …? Move around the room and invite different classmates to do things with you. Use the list of activities and phrases you wrote down in Activity F.

I. A holiday meal where I'm from. Talk to your classmates about the holiday and the meal you chose in Activity A.

1. Say what time of the year the holiday is celebrated.
2. Explain the reason for the holiday.
3. Explain who is usually present at the meal.
4. Say who usually prepares the meal.
5. Explain what dishes are served at the meal.
6. Explain any other traditions that are associated with the holiday.

J. Role plays. Your instructor will give you activity cards that you can role-play with one of your classmates. If you receive Card A, you'll invite your classmate to something. If you receive Card B, you're the person being invited and you respond accordingly. Use phrases from the **Communicative Strategies**.

K. Where R U? Young people often don't plan activities with their friends ahead of time because they can use text messages to keep up with each other. Text messaging with cell phones makes invitations very informal and immediate. Discuss with your classmates this way of socializing. How has technology changed the way people socialize? Is that a good thing?

Part Two

 PREPARE

LISTENING COMPREHENSION: *Understanding Idioms*

An *idiom* is a phrase that has an intended message that is different from its literal meaning. These phrases can be confusing for learners of English because it's not always easy to understand the intended message. For example, when someone says *He really dropped the ball on this project*, it doesn't literally mean that a ball was dropped. The intended message of this phrase is *He didn't follow through on the project* or *He made a serious mistake on this project*.

While it's probably better not to use idioms until you are more comfortable using English, it helps to understand what people are telling you. The following are some strategies for understanding idioms.

- Listen to the sentences that surround the idiom and try to guess the meaning from context.
  He's in serious trouble. *He really dropped the ball on this project*. That's going to hurt his chances for promotion. (Even if you don't know the exact meaning of the idiom, you know that *he did something wrong*.)
- If you don't understand an idiomatic phrase, ask the speaker or try to remember it so you can ask someone else. This is a strategy that works for any unknown words, phrases, or cultural references.
  ***A real team player*? I've never heard that before. What does that mean?**

CD 2 Tracks 5–12 **L.** LISTENING What does that mean? Listen to the idioms in context and underline the correct meaning from the choices given.

1. knock it off	drop it on the floor	stop it
2. twenty-four/seven	all the time	24 hours a week
3. turning over a new leaf	start something new	rake up the leaves
4. know it like the back of my hand	pretty well	really well
5. it's a piece of cake	it's sweet	it's easy
6. bend over backwards	try very hard	be flexible
7. be in the black	be unsure	make money
8. keep your chin up	keep trying	have good posture

1. What are four idiomatic phrases you hear and what they mean?

_____

_____

_____

_____

2. What are the phrases everyone uses to compliment Sandra on the dinner?

_____

_____

3. What phrases are used to talk about people?

_____

_____

4. What topics come up in this conversation?

_____

_____

Daniela: **I really like** your new hairstyle. **It's beautiful.**

Chela: **Thanks.** I like it too. I was ready for a change. Say … have you seen Carmela lately? **She looks** really **down.** I wonder what's going on.

Mia: Yeah …**she's very unhappy.** Her boyfriend broke up with her. And **I heard that he was very mean** about the whole thing. She had no idea it was going to happen.

Daniela: Well … **she's smart** and she doesn't need a guy like Marcus.

Mia: Why don't we take her out to dinner?

Chela: Good idea. **She likes** eating out. That'll distract her.

PHRASES

Bringing up Conversational Topics

You said (that) you … + *topic* + *information question*

Did you see / hear that …?

I just read / heard / saw that …

Did you catch the news today?

So, what do you think about …?

Do you like …?

Do you think …?

Do / Did you watch …?

How do you know + *name*?

You look familiar. Have we met before?

Complimenting and Responding to Compliments

Nice / Beautiful / Fabulous / Cool / Delicious / Excellent + *noun*!

Note: See the *Speaker's Handbook* on page 165 for additional phrases.

I (really) like / love your …

That is / was + *adjective*

That is / was a(n) + *noun*

You're a(n) …

My compliments! / My compliments to …

You're really good at …

Note: *You can give indirect compliments using the third person of the verb:* My mom is a fabulous cook!

Talking About People

He/She is / seems / looks + *adjective*

He/She has / doesn't have + *noun*

He/She likes / doesn't like + *verb* or *noun*

Language Focus: Small Talk

"Small talk" consists of conversational topics that are usually safe to discuss with people you don't know well.

Appropriate topics for small talk: the weather, current events (non-controversial), sports, celebrities, movies, music, surroundings, food, travel, family (non-personal), pets, hobbies

Inappropriate topics for small talk: politics, religion, salary, health, illness, death, divorce, current events (controversial), criticisms of someone, gossip, money

"Small talk" usually happens at social gatherings (parties, reunions) with people you don't know or in places where you're waiting for something (medical offices, the bus stop, waiting in line, entertainment events, etc.).

It's not polite to start small talk with people who are reading, working, talking on the phone, listening to music, using handheld devices, talking to other people, napping (on plane, train, or bus), or just sitting quietly without making eye contact.

N. What do you think about …? Write down two phrases from the **Communicative Strategies** to bring up each of the following conversational topics.

Example: baseball

Do you like baseball?

Did you see the Dodgers game last night?

1. weather

_____

_____

2. fire at the hotel

_____

_____

3. movie

_____

_____

4. pet

_____

_____

5. art exhibit

_____

_____

6. crowds at grocery store

_____

_____

O. Compliments. Make a list of six people you know (family members, friends, etc.). Then add a compliment to each name using one of the phrases from the **Communicative Strategies**.

Examples: _My brother has a really cool car._

My mother is a fantastic cook.

_____

_____

_____

_____

_____

_____

If you ever work in retail (selling merchandise) in the business world, you'll see that the Friday and Monday after Thanksgiving are the biggest shopping days of the year. These days traditionally mark the beginning of the Christmas shopping season.

On Black Friday, stores open as early as three in the morning, and people often stand in line most of the night to be the first to profit from the sales prices. The day is called "Black Friday" because it's a day when businesses are guaranteed to be "in the black," or showing a profit.

The recent growth of shopping online has led to the creation of Cyber Monday. The Monday after Thanksgiving is a day when many retailers offer great deals on products that are sold exclusively through the Internet. Delivery service providers also offer discounted and even free shipping on products that are bought on Cyber Monday.

Retailers count on the weekend after Thanksgiving as a time to make money and hope for a profitable shopping season in the weeks leading up to Christmas.

P. **Small talk.** Imagine that you're going to meet people for the first time. What can you do to prepare for the conversations? First, select some phrases you like for bringing up topics. Then make a list of topics that you wouldn't mind talking about and that might be of interest to others.

Phrases

_____

_____

_____

Topics

_____

_____

_____

 **TALK**

Q. **Peer correction.** With your classmates, compare your answers to Activities N and O. Make corrections and/or additions to your answers as necessary.

R. **Small talk.** Move around the room and use the phrases and topics you wrote down in Activity P to have conversations with your classmates. For the purposes of this activity, pretend that this is the first time you're talking to them. Be sure to say hello and to introduce yourself. Meet as many people as possible and make small talk until your instructor stops the activity.

Cultural Connections: Complimenting in the United States

Different cultures have different customs for complimenting and accepting compliments. In the United States, people are always pleased when they receive a compliment, as long as it's made sincerely. Here are some pointers to remember when giving or accepting compliments:

- Don't give too many compliments to the same person.
- It's best to compliment people on inanimate objects (e.g., car, sweater, food) and talents (e.g., a piano performance).
- In the United States, it's polite to say "Thank you" when someone compliments you.
- "Thank you" can be followed by either an acknowledgement of the praise (e.g., *I like it too.*) or a slight deflection of the praise (e.g., *It was no big deal.*).

What kinds of compliments do people give where you're from? What are the appropriate ways to respond to a compliment?

S. **Nice buffet.** Imagine that you're at a buffet dinner hosted by your boss. Start a conversation with your classmate (someone you don't know) by talking about the food that's being served. Then move on to other topics until you find a common interest with the person you're talking to. Use phrases from the **Communicative Strategies**.

T. **My favorite foods.** Talk to your classmate about your favorite foods. Mention when and where you eat them and who prepares them (compliment that person), and so forth. Use phrases from the **Communicative Strategies**.

 **IMPROVISE**

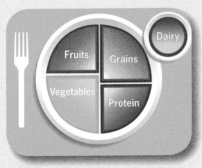

MyPlate, model for healthy eating in the United States

CD 2
Track 14

U. LISTENING Eating healthy. Listen to the nutritionist (a person who is an expert about food) talk to young people about healthy eating habits. Then answer the questions.

1. What are the three messages communicated by MyPlate?

2. According to the model, what are the two types of food we're supposed to eat the most of?

3. Which type of food and drinks should we eat (or drink) in smaller quantities?

4. Which specific examples of foods can you list for each of the major food categories? ***Fruits - Vegetables - Protein - Grains - Dairy***

5. If you follow the nutritionist's recommendations, does that mean that you never get to eat your favorite foods or sometimes eat too much?

6. What are the key words and phrases used to describe the best eating habits?

7. What are some idiomatic expressions used in the conversation and what do you think they mean?

V. Role play: Phone invitation. Pretend that you're on the phone with someone in your class. Invite the person to some event (e.g., dinner, party, barbecue, football game). Give the classmate all the details. He or she will either accept or refuse politely. If you have cell phones, you can use them to make the call. If not, turn your backs on each other. You'll also be invited by others, so be prepared to accept or refuse politely.

W. Role play: Everything is delicious! Pretend that you and several classmates are at the dinner table, talking about the food, making small talk, complimenting the hosts, etc. Decide ahead of time who the hosts are and who the guests are.

X. Role play: Thanks for inviting us. With the same classmates as in Activity W, role-play the scene when you're leaving the house. Thank the hosts, compliment them again, talk about a possible next time you might get together, remind someone of something, and finally say goodbye.

Y. A multi-national dinner. With your classmates, plan a class dinner that includes dishes from different cultures. Plan all the details of the dinner (when, where, who, what) and decide which classmates you'll ask to bring different dishes representing their cultures. Also decide if spouses, boyfriends, girlfriends, and other people will be invited.

INTERNET RESEARCH U.S. holidays. Go online and find an American holiday (official or unofficial) you think is particularly interesting. Some examples: July 4th, Memorial Day, Labor Day, Thanksgiving, Christmas, Hanukkah, Kwanzaa, New Year's Eve, Passover, Ramadan, Cinco de Mayo, Patriots' Day, Veterans' Day, Halloween, Earth Day, Mother's Day, Father's Day, Groundhog Day, Valentine's Day, April Fool's Day. Find out what the holiday means, what customs and foods are associated with it, and report back to your classmates about what you found out.

4 A Family Get-together

"When are we all getting together?"

Strategies for Communication

Part 1: How to Make Plans
Part 2: How to Talk About People

●● PREPARE ●●

A. PRE-LISTENING Planning a family get-together. Imagine that you're in charge of planning a three-day family get-together for your extended family. Check (✓) the things that you would need to do. Put an ✗ next to the items that would not apply to your situation. You may write your own ideas for the last two items.

_____ make flight arrangements for relatives coming from far away

_____ decide who will attend the event

_____ figure out where the get-together will be held

_____ provide train schedules for family members arriving by train

_____ contact all the relatives to determine the best dates for the get-together

_____ send out invitations

_____ decide who will make follow-up phone calls to relatives

_____ pick people up from the airport

_____ make hotel reservations

_____ figure out where everyone will be staying

_____ pick people up from the train station

_____ decide on the menus for meals

_____ decide if it's going to be potluck or catered or both

_____ ask other family members to help with the planning

_____ plan activities for the children

_____ make arrangements for music

_____ figure out what the teenagers could do for fun

_____ figure out the cost of the get-together

_____ find out how much each family is willing to contribute financially

_____ make specific plans for each day (e.g., meal times, activities)

_____ buy decorations (balloons, streamers, etc.)

_____ buy a gift for the oldest member of your family

_____ decide who will do the cooking and/or grilling

_____ ask friends or neighbors to take care of your pets during the days of the event

_____ hire someone to clean the house the week before the get-together

_____ rent a party tent for the backyard in case it rains

_____ rent chairs and tables

_____ buy paper plates, plastic utensils, napkins, tablecloths

_____ _____

_____ _____

Cultural Connections: Family Reunions

In the United States, families frequently organize large family reunions as a way to stay connected with each other. Families often live far apart, and reunions may bring together people from different parts of the country by car, bus, train, and even plane. Usually one family is in charge of organizing the reunion, but all families contribute time or money to it. A reunion can last from one to three days and may include parties, picnics, barbecues, short excursions to nearby sites, and activities for children and young people. Family reunions generally happen no more than once a year and may be organized every several years.

Family reunions give relatives of all generations a chance to stay in touch or get reacquainted with other members of an extended family. Young people get to meet cousins, aunts, and uncles, while older members get to see grandchildren, nieces, and nephews.

It's assumed that family reunions became a custom when extended families no longer lived in the same homes, neighborhoods, and towns. In a country as large as the United States, spread-out families could lose touch with each other. While social media, e-mail, phone calls, and texting make it easier for families to share news, the reunion remains a tradition for many families in all parts of the country.

For what reasons do families get together where you're from? Who organizes these events? Who participates? What foods and activities are planned?

CD 2 🔊))
Tracks
15–18

B. LISTENING A family reunion. You'll hear four short descriptions. Write the letter of each description under the appropriate picture.

1. _____

2. _____

3. _____

4. _____

CD 2 Tracks 19–20 **C.** LISTENING The details of the reunion. The two organizers of the family reunion have finished planning. One is in charge of the calendar and the other decides who will do what. As you listen to the two explanations, (1) put the events into the calendar, and then (2) write down what each person has agreed to do (four tasks per person).

1.

Friday, June 11	Saturday, June 12	Sunday, June 13
9:00 _____	9:00 _____	9:00 _____
10:00 _____	10:00 _____	10:00 _____
11:00 _____	11:00 _____	11:00 _____
12:00 _____	12:00 _____	12:00 _____
01:00 _____	01:00 _____	01:00 _____
02:00 _____	02:00 _____	02:00 _____
03:00 _____	03:00 _____	03:00 _____
04:00 _____	04:00 _____	04:00 _____
05:00 _____	05:00 _____	05:00 _____
06:00 _____	06:00 _____	06:00 _____
07:00 _____	07:00 _____	07:00 _____
08:00 _____	08:00 _____	08:00 _____

2.

Aunt Beth
_____
_____
_____
_____

Uncle Rick
_____
_____
_____
_____

Cousin Alex
_____
_____
_____
_____

Grandpa Sid
_____
_____
_____
_____

Grandma Cynthia
_____
_____
_____
_____

Language Focus: Reduced Form: *Gonna*

The reduced form **gonna (going to)** can be used only with another verb to indicate future time.

Alex is **gonna (going to) rent** the tent. (He hasn't done it yet, but will do so.)

Gonna can *never* be used with a noun to show movement from one place to another. To indicate movement, **going to** + *destination* is required.

I'm **going to** the train station.

D. Planning an activity. Jot down three or four phrases that you might use to do each of the following things.

1. Asking someone to do something _____

_____

2. Delegating tasks _____

_____

3. Making suggestions _____

_____

4. Asking for information _____

_____

COMMUNICATIVE STRATEGIES: *How to Make Plans*

Sam:	So **who's going to do what**?
Cecilia:	Wait! **First things first. We need** a date and a place for the party before we decide **who's doing what**.
Eric:	I thought we had already decided on the date.
Mateo:	No, **that's still up in the air.**
Cecilia:	**Why don't we** make it two weeks from Saturday.
Sam:	**That's fine with me.** What about the rest of you?
Mateo:	**Hmm … I'm not sure.** Does that give us enough time?
Eric:	**Sure.** If we all pitch in to help.

PHRASES

Starting the Planning

What are we going to do?
Who's going to do what?
to go back to the drawing board (to start all over again)
first things first (do the most important thing first)
That's still up in the air (it hasn't been decided yet)
to make up one's mind (to make a decision)

Making Suggestions

Why don't we …?
Why not …?
I'd really like to …
How about …?
Should we …?
Would you like to …?
What would you say to …?
Why can't we …?
We may / could / might …
And then (maybe / possibly) …
Maybe we should / could …
We need …

Responding to Suggestions

Good thinking! / Good idea!
I'd rather not …
Why not?
I'm not sure.
Sure. That sounds good.
Hmm … That's a lot of / too much trouble.
Not really. I'd rather …
That's fine with me. / I'm OK with that.
That's a possibility.
That sounds like a plan.
Good point.

E. What are the appropriate responses? For each suggestion, write down two responses and suggestions that make sense. Select phrases from the **Communicative Strategies**. Give reasons for your reactions.

Example: We could hold the neighborhood party on the 22nd.

> **A:**   That's fine with me. I'll be back from my business trip by then.
>
> **B:**   I'm not sure. That's a holiday weekend. A lot of people are on vacation.

1. Why don't we rent the community center for the class reunion?

_____

_____

2. Why not have a picnic in the park?

_____

_____

3. How about we surprise our parents with a trip to Russia? We'd plan the whole thing.

_____

_____

4. How about organizing a welcome home party for Liu? She's getting home from Brazil in a few weeks.

_____

_____

5. Why can't we just have a simple barbecue instead of this complicated event?

_____

_____

6. Maybe we should hold the next reunion at a ski resort.

_____

_____

7. What would you say to a party at the beach?

_____

_____

8. I'd really like to organize a reunion of our high school friends.

_____

_____

◗◗ TALK ◗◗

F. Peer correction.   Compare your list from Activity D with that of your classmates. Add any phrases that you find interesting or helpful.

G. Role play: Planning a reunion.   Based on your answers in Activity A and using the expressions from Activity D and the **Communicative Strategies**, plan a family reunion with your classmates. Select the tasks that are appropriate to your situation and decide on the logistics: when, who, what, etc.

H. Role play: The logistics of the reunion.   You're the designated person to report back to the class about what you decided to do for your reunion (Activity G). As you explain what you'll do, other members of your group can provide additional details.

I. Planning a birthday party.   You and your classmates are organizing a surprise birthday party for one of the people in your class. Decide when and where it will be, who will be invited, what food and drink you'll serve, who will buy the food and drinks, who will prepare the food, etc.

Example: **A:** *Let's organize a surprise birthday party for Sakura.*
B: *Good idea! When's her birthday?*
A: *It's a week from Saturday.*
C: *Good. That gives us plenty of time to plan.*
D: *Yes, but we have to be really careful so she doesn't suspect anything.*
B: *We could have the party at my house. I'd be happy to prepare the food if one of you helps me.*
C: *Sure. That sounds good. I can do the shopping. …*

Language Focus: Using *go* to Indicate Movement and Activity

When you ask people for help, assign tasks, or volunteer for tasks in organizing a project or event, you may use **go** with another verb to indicate both movement and an activity:

Could you **go talk** to him?
He could **go get** the flowers.
She'll **go pick up** the kids at school.

When using the past tense **went**, the verb that follows is in the infinitive form:

She **went to pick up** the kids at school.
He **went to get** the flowers.

J. So how was the birthday party?   Everyone went to Sakura's surprise birthday party. Tell your instructor about it. Give a very detailed description (when, where, who, food, music, activities, gifts, etc.).

●● PREPARE ●●

LISTENING COMPREHENSION: *Inferences made from level and tone of voice (non-verbal communication)*

Level and tone of voice can tell you a lot about the general tone of the conversation as well as the speakers' attitudes. For example, with the help of tone, gestures, posture, facial expressions, and a few words, you might be able to decide that the speaker is expressing regret, happiness, anger, surprise, criticism, indifference, or some other feelings.

- Speaking loudly in a strident tone of voice may indicate anger, irritation, boasting, rudeness, a desire to call attention to yourself, or a desire to be heard by everyone present. It may also simply be a strategy used to be heard in a noisy place.
- Speaking softly or whispering can suggest secrets, gossip, a desire not to be overheard, a desire to be polite, or a desire not to call attention to yourself.

Cultural Connections: Voice and Gestures

- In the United States, crossing one's arms during a conversation is a defensive posture that suggests unwillingness to listen to other points of view.
- In Thailand, two people who whisper to each other in the company of other people are considered impolite. (This is also true in most cultures.)
- In China, it is considered unacceptable to show emotion through tone (level) of voice or gestures.
- In Argentina, placing your hands on your hips during a conversation means that you're angry.
- In Indonesia, using a loud voice is considered aggressive. Indonesians usually speak in hushed, subdued tones.

What are some of the customs associated with voice and gestures where you're from? What non-verbal communication is considered polite or impolite?

CD 2 ◀))) **K.** LISTENING Did you hear? Write the letter of the conversation above the appropriate
Tracks   drawing. Then write down the topic of the conversation and some key words that helped
21–26   you recognize it.

1. _____

Topic: _____
Key words:

_____ _____

_____ _____

2. _____

Topic: _____
Key words:

_____ _____

_____ _____

3. _____

Topic: _____
Key words:

_____ _____

_____ _____

4. _____

Topic: _____
Key words:

_____   _____

_____   _____

5. _____

Topic: _____
Key words:

_____   _____

_____   _____

6. _____

Topic: _____
Key words:

_____   _____

_____   _____

CD 2 🔊))
Tracks
21–26

L. **LISTENING Did you hear?** Listen again to the conversations from Activity K. For each conversation check (✔) if the conversation is or is not gossip. Then write down the feelings expressed by the tone of voice and words used by the speakers.

	GOSSIP	NOT GOSSIP	FEELINGS EXPRESSED (criticism, happiness, anger, surprise, compassion)
Conversation 1			
Conversation 2			
Conversation 3			
Conversation 4			
Conversation 5			
Conversation 6			

COMMUNICATIVE STRATEGIES: *How to Talk About People*

Adam: **Did you hear that** Eric's father kicked him out of the house?
Zachary: That's ridiculous. Why are people **constantly** making up stories! **I talked to** Eric's sister and all that **got into an argument** and Eric **lost his temper.**
Adam: So **do you think** Eric is still living at home?
Zachary: Of course. He just invited me to go watch the football game with him and his father.

Rumors / Gossip / Invented Story

I heard that …

Did you hear that …?

I saw …

Do you think …?

I read somewhere that …

Somebody on TV / on the radio said that …

What do you think …?

Rumor has it that …

Someone told me that …

In my opinion, …

He/she seems …

Factual Information

I talked to …

She called me and told me …

Several studies have shown that …

My wife / child / husband doesn't like …

He + *what the person does / did / will do*

According to the paper, the (event) will …

I'm planning a party (*or other activity*).

Her birthday is …

The weather …

Exaggerations / Generalizations

every time

whenever

always

constantly

never

You don't care about what I think / say /
  want / need / *etc.*

All you care about is …

Fights and Arguments

to get into a fight (argument)

to lose one's temper

to tell someone off

to stab someone in the back

to butt into someone's business

to take something the wrong way

to give someone the cold shoulder

to treat someone like dirt

to get on someone's nerves

to freak out (*slang*)

to be hot under the collar

Professional Context: Gossip in Business and Academia

Most gossip involves negative comments and criticism and implies feelings of superiority over the person being talked about. Therefore, gossip and rumors should be avoided altogether in professional settings. Many cultures view gossip negatively and even actively discourage it. However, it is human nature to talk about other people without necessarily knowing all the facts.

In business and academia, you should *never* gossip:
- to anyone about a boss, professor, or superior;
- about colleagues or other students to a boss, professor, or superior; and
- about your current employer or institution to a possible future employer or institution (e.g., in an interview). This can lead to mistrust in you that you might do the same thing if you are employed by the new institution in the future.

M. Rumor or fact? Decide whether each statement or question is rumor or fact. Place a check (✓) in the appropriate box.

		RUMOR	FACT
1.	Do you think they're getting a divorce?		
2.	My sister told me she got a promotion.		
3.	Ali seems a bit down lately. I wonder what's going on.		
4.	I heard that Alicia is thinking of moving.		
5.	My kids absolutely hate vegetables. I don't know what to do.		
6.	I saw Joshua with a new girl. What do you know about that?		
7.	It snowed all day yesterday. I stayed at home and read all day.		
8.	According to the paper, the concert starts at 8:00.		
9.	I read on the Internet that this herb isn't good for you.		

CD 2 Tracks 27–32   **N.** LISTENING What are they arguing about? Listen to the disagreements. Make a list of reasons that the people are arguing.

Reasons for Arguments (Topics)

1. _____
2. _____
3. _____
4. _____
5. _____
6. _____

Language Focus: The Preposition *like*

The preposition **like** can be used to introduce an example (place, people, things) of something that has just been mentioned.
A: *Would you consider holding the reunion at a more interesting place next time?* **Like** *maybe at an ocean resort?*
B: *Good idea!* **Like** *in California or maybe Florida or South Carolina.*
C: *Or maybe* **like** *the South of France or Hawaii or the coast of Brazil!*

CD 2 🔊 **O.** LISTENING **Family spat.** Family reunions can be tense. Listen to the argument and
Track 33   then answer the questions.

1. What is the relationship among the three family members?

_____

2. What are Chris and the teenager fighting about?

_____

_____

3. What does Chris want the teenager to do?

_____

4. Why does Chris think he can tell the teenager what to do?

_____

5. Why do you think that Chris is so extremely angry with the teenager?

_____

6. What solution does Chris propose so that everyone will be happier at this reunion?

_____

7. What does Chris propose for the next family reunion?

_____

8. What does the family have to do in order to approve of Chris's proposal for the next
reunion?

_____

9. In the context of this conversation, what do you think the following idioms mean?
   a. Knock it off! _____
   b. to put up with _____
   c. Let's face it! _____
   d. to be crazy about _____
   e. It's a thought. _____
   f. Fat chance! _____
   g. to catch up with each other _____

P. What about you? List the reasons why you've had arguments with other people.

Example: _arguments with my friend about eating meat / I'm a vegetarian_

_____

_____

_____

_____

TALK

Q. Peer correction. Compare your answers to the items in Activities M, N, and O with those of your classmates. In Activities N and O your answers may be somewhat different. If you disagree in Activity M, look at the items again and explain how you arrived at your answers.

R. What about you? Compare your list from Activity P with those of your classmates. Do arguments generally occur with the same people (friends, family members, strangers, superiors, vendors, etc.)? Do you and your classmates tend to argue about the same things or are your topics very different?

S. Role play: An argument. With a classmate, play out one of the arguments you put on your list in Activity P. Then switch and use one of the situations on your partner's list.

T. Talking about people. Talking about people does not necessarily mean gossiping or saying bad things about them. It may just mean describing what they are like, their appearance, what their interests are, etc. With a classmate, look at the pictures and describe the people, inventing as much as you can about them based on what you see.

⚫⚫ IMPROVISE ⚫⚫

U. **The rumor game.** Your instructor will tell you a story about an imaginary person. You go to someone else and repeat the story. This person then goes to someone else and retells the rumor. When five or six of you have repeated the rumor, you'll be asked to compare the original story with the final rumor.

V. **Rumors and gossip.** With your classmates, look again at the drawings of the people in Activity T. This time, you take turns inventing stories about them (good or bad, but not nasty!). The others in your group explain why the rumors are probably untrue and try to convince you not to spread them around.

W. **A family tradition.** Think of a gathering that has taken place in your family, such as a wedding, the birth of a child, a holiday (secular or religious), a reunion, a vacation, a birthday, an anniversary, a seasonal celebration, etc. What kind of planning did it take? Include details of decorations, special menu, activities, invitations, and so on. Tell your classmates about it.

X. **My relationships with others.** Talk to your classmates about your relationship with a family member or a friend. Tell them about how often you interact with each other and under what circumstances, what you argue about, when you've been angry with the person, what you have in common, what activities you like to do together, etc.

> **Example:** **A:** *I get along really well with my brother, but my sister and I always seem to get on each other's nerves.*
> **B:** *So what irritates you about your sister?*
> **A:** *Well, both my sister and I are very competitive about the same things.*
> **C:** *Isn't your brother competitive?*
> **A:** *Sure. But not about the same things that I care about …*

INTERNET RESEARCH Reunions and Get-togethers. Research an interesting tradition that brings people together in your culture or in another culture (e.g., Chinese New Year, Thanksgiving in the United States, etc.). What activities are associated with this tradition that require a considerable amount of planning and work (special food and drink, decorations, activities, etc.)? Describe the tradition to your classmates using the phrases you learned in this chapter.

5 A Meeting with the Advisor

"I could use your advice."

Strategies for Communication

Part 1: How to Ask for and Respond to Advice

Part 2: How to Talk about Problems

Part One

PREPARE

A. PRE-LISTENING Choosing courses. Read the college course descriptions and answer the questions that follow.

COLPREP 105. How to Succeed in College. Focus on intermediate and advanced reading comprehension, note-taking skills, outlining and organizing papers, participating in class discussions and making oral presentations, taking tests, and improving research skills. Prerequisites: None.

BIO 200. Introduction to Physiology. Introduction to the principles of how the human body functions. Focus on cells, tissues, and organs. This course is a prerequisite for more advanced study in any health-related field. Prerequisites: BIO 100.

ECON 110. Contemporary Issues in American Economics. Discussion of economic decision-making. Possible topics: whether or not to protect domestic markets from foreign competition; the environmental impact of manufacturing practices; the future of the U.S. Social Security system; health care in the United States. Prerequisites: Appropriate Math Placement Test of 300 or permission of instructor.

ENG 101. The American Short Story. Survey of the American short story, including Nathaniel Hawthorn, Edgar Allen Poe, Samuel L. Clemens (Mark Twain), William Sydney Porter (O. Henry) and Joyce Carol Oates. Focuses on basic analysis of literature, on the classic form of the

short story, and on what makes this literature uniquely American. Prerequisite: ENG 75.

HIST 102. American History after the Civil War. Course topics include the impact of industrial and agricultural revolutions on U.S. society, culture, and government. Analysis of United States' participation in World Wars I and II and of the impact on the United States of the 20th century's major social, economic, political, and cultural movements. Prerequisite: None.

MATH 150. Precalculus. Designed to prepare students for calculus and other advanced mathematics courses. Course includes advanced algebra and trigonometry, functions, analytic geometry, and trigonometry. Prerequisites: MATH 100 or appropriate Math Placement Test score.

PHIL 150. Ethics. Examination of the concept of "moral judgment." Readings include classical and contemporary philosophical texts, and modern texts on ethics. Discussion-based course. Prerequisite: None.

PSYCH 250. Abnormal Psychology. Introductory course on the field of abnormal psychology with special emphasis placed on strategies for behavioral change, concepts relating to community mental health, and cross-cultural comparisons of approaches to treatment. Prerequisites: PSYCH 150 (Introduction to Psychology).

---

1. Are any of these courses similar to ones you've taken?

_____

_____

2. Which of the courses do you think would be the most interesting or enjoyable for you? Explain.

_____

_____

3. Which course do you think would be the hardest for you? Explain.

_____

_____

4. Which course do you think might have the least reading? The most reading?

_____

_____

5. Would you be eligible to register for Abnormal Psychology for next term? Why or why not?

_____

_____

6. If you were going to take three of these courses in the same term, which three would you choose? Explain.

_____

_____

CD 2 Tracks 34–39 **B.** LISTENING **What's that class like?** Listen to the conversations. For each, place an X on the line to show your interpretation of what the speaker says about the course.

Example: You hear:

> **A:** *Wow, did you see how many books there are for your English class? Six!! I'll bet they cost a fortune.*
>
> **B:** *Well, they're sure not cheap. But my marketing books cost twice as much as those.*

You mark:
English books
Inexpensive ——————————X—————— Expensive

1. Web Design

Useful / Relevant ————————————————— Not useful / Irrelevant

2. Intro to Psychology

Student friendly ————————————— Demanding
Even workload   Uneven workload

3. Astronomy

Interesting ————————————— Boring

4. American History II

Difficult ————————————— Easy

5. Cultural Anthropology

Mostly group work ————————————— Mostly independent work

6. Art and Culture in the 20th Century

Mostly creative work ————————————— Mostly lecture, reading

In the United States, secondary schools and universities have advisors who help students succeed in school and make plans for the future. In middle school and high school, one of the main functions of a guidance counselor is to help students choose colleges that are right for them, and then guide them through the application process.

At the college level, an academic advisor helps students select their courses and gives them advice about choosing a major, studying abroad, and applying for jobs and internships. Advisors also try to make sure their first-year advisees make a smooth transition to college life.

Although not always the case, some students keep the same advisor for their entire college career. They may eventually feel comfortable asking for advice about slightly more personal problems.

Do secondary and college students have advisors where you're from? If so, what is their role? If not, who would students go to for advice about academic or personal issues?

CD 2 🔊 **C.** LISTENING What should I take? Listen to this excerpt of a conversation between a
Track 40   student and her advisor. Then answer the questions that follow.

1. Who is Maria? Do you think it's her first term in college? Explain your answer. What is her probable major?

_____

_____

_____

2. Check (✓) the three courses Maria will take next term.

_____ American Short Story   _____ How to Succeed in College

_____ Business Statistics   _____ Math 120

_____ Contemporary   _____ Shakespeare
                Issues in Economics

3. Which courses does the advisor think are right for Maria? Indicate whether the advisor approves of each course, and explain why.

Course: **American Short Story**

Does the advisor approve of the choice?   Yes   No

Why or why not? _____

_____

Course: **Business Statistics**

Does the advisor approve of the choice?   Yes   No

Why or why not? _____

_____

Course: **Contemporary Issues in Economics**

Does the advisor approve of the choice?   Yes   No

Why or why not? _____

_____

Course: **How to Succeed in College**

Does the advisor approve of the choice?   Yes   No

Why or why not? _____

_____

Course: **Math 120**

Does the advisor approve of the choice?   Yes   No

Why or why not? _____

_____

Course: **Shakespeare**

Does the advisor approve of the choice?   Yes   No

Why or why not? _____

_____

4. Do you think Maria accepts her advisor's opinions? Write down some of the things

Maria says that support your answer. _____

_____

_____

COMMUNICATIVE STRATEGIES: *How to Ask for and Respond to Advice*

Anna: **Thanks** for reading over my paper. **What do you think** about it?

George: Well … **in my opinion,** it still needs some work. The transitions aren't always clear, and the conclusion isn't as good as it could be. **Have you considered** taking it to the Writing Center? They're always really helpful.

Anna: Hmm, **that's a good idea.**

George: And **I think that if you go over it** with them, **you'll end up** with an even better paper.

PHRASES

Asking for / Responding to Advice or Opinions	Offering Advice
What do / did you think?	(I think / don't think) You should …
(So,) (Do) You think I can / should …?	Have you considered / thought about …?
So, you're suggesting that?	I'd like you to …
Is it / Would it be a good idea to …?	If I were you, I'd / I wouldn't …
Who / What / When / Where / How …?	There are lots of advantages / benefits to …
Thanks for the suggestion / the advice.	If you …, you …
That makes a lot of sense.	You may regret it if you …
That's a good idea.	It would be a good idea to …
I see what you're saying …	You might consider / want to …
I'm gonna have to think it over …	

Stating Preferences	Stating Opinions
I (really) like / don't like …	In my opinion / view …
I'm (not) really interested in …	I (don't) think / believe / feel …
I don't (really) want to …	Here's what I'd say:
I think / don't think I'd like to …	If you ask me …
I / I'd prefer …	

Note: See the *Speaker's Handbook,* page 165 for additional phrases.

D. I'll think about it. Write two responses to each of the pieces of advice an advisor might give a student. Use phrases from the **Communicative Strategies** and other phrases you already know.

Example: I think you ought to take at least one science course while you're here.

    a. I guess you're right … Is Intro to Psych considered a science course?

    b. I know. I really want to, actually. But I want to take Astronomy 101, and that's not offered 'til next term.

1. I'm afraid the philosophy seminar might be a bit too difficult for you at this point.

    a. _____

    b. _____

2. You've done really well in your history courses. You might want to major in history.

a. _____

b. _____

3. If I were you, I'd ask the prof to go over your last test with you. That would help you understand what kinds of answers he's looking for.

a. _____

b. _____

4. There are lots of advantages to taking an American literature class.

a. _____

b. _____

5. I think you might regret it later if you drop that course now.

a. _____

b. _____

E. **How do I handle this?** Write down two questions a student might ask an advisor to get his or her advice.

Example: You're having a problem with a roommate.

a. *How do I ask him not to make so much noise after 11:00?*

b. *Should I ask the Housing Office to let me change roommates?*

1. You want to get into a class that's full.

a. _____

b. _____

2. You're thinking about transferring to another school.

a. _____

b. _____

3. You want to do an internship next summer.

a. _____

b. _____

4. You think it would be cool to take an art class, but you've never had one before.

a. _____

b. _____

5. You're supposed to give a group presentation with some classmates, and the group isn't working very well together.

a. _____

b. _____

F. **My courses.** List two courses you're taking now or have taken (invent some classes, if necessary). Make some notes about the professors, the kinds of assignments you have, the books you're reading, etc. Note whether you'd advise another student to take these classes. Then write one or two questions you could ask a classmate to get some advice—either about some difficulties you're having or about courses you're considering for next term. Use phrases from the **Communicative Strategies**.

Language Focus: Making Advice and Criticism Seem Less Rude

When giving advice or offering criticism, you can make your remarks seem less critical by adding words or phrases containing adjectives and adverbs.

Compare: This essay is disorganized. It's not clear. You should rework it.

With: In my opinion, your essay seems **rather** disorganized. It's not **quite** clear **enough. Maybe** you should rework it **some more.**

Compare: This dinner is unappetizing. There's no salt in anything, and everything is the same color.

With: This dinner's gonna be good. All it needs is a **little** bit of salt, and then **maybe** some parsley or lettuce to add **some** color.

 TALK

G. **Peer correction.** Compare your answers to Activities D and E with those of your classmates. Make corrections and additions to your answers as necessary.

H. **My courses.** Using the information you wrote down in Activity F, tell a classmate about your courses. Explain what they're about, what you like and dislike about them, and whether you would advise others to take them. Then ask your classmate for advice about any difficulties you might be having in the classes or about what classes to take next term. When you've finished, switch roles. Use phrases from the **Communicative Strategies** and keep the conversation going.

I. **Role-plays: Here's what I'd suggest.** With a partner, role-play situations described in the Activity Cards your instructor gives you. Create a natural-sounding conversation. Use phrases from the **Communicative Strategies** and fill in the details.

J. **It's up to you …** Play the roles of a student and an academic advisor discussing whether it's wise to take a certain course the student is interested in. You may use a few of the ideas given below as a way of getting started. Use phrases from the **Communicative Strategies** for asking, giving and responding to advice, and keep the conversation going.

Possible topics:

Why you want to take the course: You like the teacher, you love the subject, you think it would give you an advantage on the job market, you like to be challenged, etc.

Why you're concerned: The course might be too advanced, there might be too much reading, you may not have had the prerequisite or its equivalent, other students in the class may be more advanced than you, etc.

Advisor suggests how to decide whether course is appropriate: Talk with the prof during office hours, get a copy of the syllabus, go to the bookstore and look at the books for the course, ask students who've already taken it, read some articles about the topic, etc.

Advisor asks questions to help you decide: Think about what other courses you'll be taking, are you sure you'll have time to study enough, are you very motivated, might you attend for first couple of days to see what it's like, have you been successful in other difficult courses, etc.

Example: **A:**   *Hi, Professor Smith, do you have a moment?*
            B: *Sure, Michelle, what's up?*
            A: *Well, there's this course I'm really interested in, but I need your advice. I'm wondering if it would be too hard for me.*
            B: *Well, let's take a look at the course description and the prerequisites you're supposed to have …*

Professional Context: Academic Preparation for the Job Market

While you're in school, you should definitely choose courses that prepare you for the kind of job you'd like to have, but don't forget to take a certain number of general education courses as well. Managers appreciate employees who can speak and write clearly and who are willing to learn new things. Most of them also like to see some breadth as well as depth in the courses you've taken.

Once you've started working, your education may not be finished. Many companies provide on-the-job training in technical skills, computer software use, sales techniques, etc. In addition, employers may offer to pay your tuition to continue your education if they think it would be useful for your job, or if they're thinking of promoting you.

Part Two

 **PREPARE** ●●

LISTENING COMPREHENSION: *Interpreting Indirect Messages*

American speech has a reputation for being quite direct. However, some people choose to communicate ideas indirectly in certain situations. Indirect communication often happens when people are hesitant about contradicting others, giving them a direct order, criticizing them, or giving them advice. Listen for these ways that people may send messages indirectly.

- They may ask *leading questions* (questions that are asked in a way that pushes you toward the answer they want to hear, or that indicates what they want you to do).
- They may suggest that what you're doing is unusual, thereby hinting that your way is not correct, not a good way to proceed. This may involve stressing a certain word to suggest that something is not quite right. ("That's *interesting* . . . ," "I think you're *mostly* right," etc.)
- They may tell you what they want by suggesting that it's what you want. ("Well, you must be anxious to get home.")

CD 2 🔊))) **K.** LISTENING Can you take a hint? In each of these short conversations, the first
Tracks   speaker is communicating an indirect message. Indicate whether you think the second
41–48   speaker understood this message and, if not, what you think he or she should have said
           or done.

Example: You hear:
   A: It's *awfully* cold in here, isn't it?
   B: Yes, it is. Would you like me to close that window?

You circle: (Message understood)   Message not understood

1. Message understood   Message not understood

_____

2. Message understood   Message not understood

_____

3. Message understood   Message not understood

_____

4. Message understood   Message not understood

_____

5. Message understood   Message not understood

_____

6. Message understood   Message not understood

_____

7. Message understood   Message not understood

_____

8. Message understood   Message not understood

_____

CD 2
Track 49 **L.** **LISTENING Helpful advice.** Listen to the conversation between Marco and Rita, a family friend. Then answer the questions that follow.

1. What's the main piece of advice Rita is giving Marco?

_____

2. Do you think Rita had intended to say something about Marco's lateness, or do you think it just came up naturally in the conversation? Explain your answer.

_____

_____

3. Rita uses some indirect ways to get to the point. How does she steer the subject toward what she wants to discuss?

_____

_____

4. What does she finally say to make her point very clear?

_____

_____

5. How good would you say Marco is at understanding indirect messages? Explain your answer.

_____

_____

COMMUNICATIVE STRATEGIES: *How to Talk about Problems*

A: Sorry if I'm acting weird. **I'm really upset** right now.

B: That's too bad. Do you want to talk about it?

A: Well, the workers started repairing the storm damage to our kitchen roof, but now they've disappeared. I don't know when they'll be back.

B: That's awful. Is there anything I can do to help?

A: I don't think so, but thanks a lot for the offer—really.

B: Well, **what if I** bring you some dinner for the next couple of nights? I'd be happy to do that.

A: That would be so wonderful. You're such a good friend!

PHRASES

Talking about a Problem

Nothing is going right. / Everything is going wrong.

I'm (so) frustrated / annoyed / upset / angry.

I've got a problem / problems with …

No matter how hard I try, I can't (seem to / manage to) …

I can't handle …

I don't know what I'm going to do / how I'm going to …

I can't decide / make up my mind.

I can't take it anymore.

Responding to Someone with a Problem

What's up? / What's the matter?

I'm sorry to hear that.

Do you want to talk about it?

Oh, no. That's too bad / terrible / awful.

What are you gonna do?

Have you thought about …?

Maybe you should / could …

Maybe it's not as bad as you think.

Is there anything I can do to help you?

What if I …?

Try not to worry.

I'm sure things will work out / be all right.

Speaking Hypothetically

What would happen (if) …?

What if …?

Do you think (maybe) (it's because) … ?

Why do you think …?

If + *simple past*, [then] + I / we, *etc.* would / could / might + *verb*

If + *the past perfect*, [then] I / we, *etc.* would have / could have / might have + *past participle*

Should I (have) …?

Do you think I should (have) …?

(Let's) suppose / say / assume / imagine that …

I wonder / I imagine / I suspect …

Talking about the Future

Can you predict …?

What (do you think) will happen (if …)?

Do you think …?

Soon / Someday / In (the next) ten years / In / By 2050 / Never, *etc.*

It's possible / probable / obvious / certain (*etc.*) that …

I'll / we'll / they'll (*etc.*) probably / definitely / never / always, *etc.*

If + present tense, (then) + future …

There's no chance / a good chance …

That's bound to / That may well happen.

Note: See the *Speaker's Handbook*, page 165 for additional phrases.

M. What's the matter? Each of the people mentioned below is having a problem and is talking it over with a friend. Write short dialogues in which one speaker talks about the problem, and the other responds appropriately. Vary the phrases you use from the **Communication Strategies.**

Example: a parent who's having problems with a child

    A: Have you got time to talk? I am so frustrated!

    B: Why? What's the matter?

    A: I just can't get Hilary to eat properly. All she wants is pasta.

    B: Oh, she'll get over it. A lot of kids go through that phase. Try not to worry.

1. a parent who's having problems with a child

    A: _____

    B: _____

    A: _____

    B: _____

2. a person who had an accident last weekend, and whose arm is broken

    A: _____

    B: _____

    A: _____

    B: _____

3. a young adult who has to choose between two job offers

    A: _____

    B: _____

    A: _____

    B: _____

4. a friend whose computer was stolen

    A: _____

    B: _____

    A: _____

    B: _____

N. Consequences. Complete these exchanges in which one person predicts or imagines the consequences of an action the other one is considering. Use a variety of the phrases you know for hypothesizing and predicting.

Example: Do you think it would be OK if I bought Tommy a drum?

    If you did that, I think his parents would never speak to you again.

1. Do you think it'll be OK if I bring Chris home to meet my parents?

_____

2. Would it be so bad if I dropped out of school?

_____

3. What if I miss my 8:30 class a few more times? I keep oversleeping, but it's a big class—maybe the prof won't notice.

_____

4. Do you think I could just find something on the Internet instead of writing the paper myself?

_____

5. If I forgot your birthday, what would you do?

_____

6. If I don't show up at their wedding, do you think they'll forgive me?

_____

O. Lots to do … Make a detailed list of the activities you do in a typical week, and about how much time you spend doing them. You'll share this information with a classmate later.

_____

_____

_____

_____

_____

_____

_____

_____

Cultural Connections: Extracurricular Activities

From elementary school through college, American students can participate in a wide variety of extracurricular activities. When these activities are sponsored and organized by the school, they usually take place before or after school or on weekends. Some school-sponsored extracurricular activities include sports, theater, music, clubs (French club, chess club, etc.), community service projects, science, math, or debate competitions, model United Nations, etc.

Such activities are important to many students. In high school, for instance, playing football might be what keeps a reluctant student in school, or acting in a school play might increase a shy student's confidence. In addition, colleges often consider students' participation in such activities when deciding which ones to admit. Extracurricular activities allow students to take a break from their studies, pursue other interests, and construct more balanced lives.

However, students who become too involved in extracurricular activities can see their academic performance decline. Students need to learn to create a balance between work (or studying), extracurricular activities, and their personal lives.

Do schools and universities organize extracurricular activities for students where you're from? How else do students get involved in organized sports, groups, or volunteer work?

TALK

P. Peer correction. Show a classmate the dialogues you wrote for Activities M and N, and decide which ones you like best. Help each other make any necessary corrections.

Q. Lots to do … Using the notes you took in Activity O, talk with a classmate about your schedule. Give each other advice about time management, and hypothesize about how you might organize your lives better, etc.

R. Future plans. With a classmate, have a conversation about your future plans. If you could be, have, or do anything you wanted, what would it be? What are you doing now to prepare for the future? What problems or obstacles are you facing? What advice have your advisor, friends, or family given you? Your classmate will ask questions, give you advice, make hypotheses about the future, encourage you, etc.

S. Extracurricular activities. With a classmate, discuss the concept of extracurricular activities. What is their purpose, as you understand it? What activities do you know about, and which ones do you find most interesting? Do you see some as being more valuable than others? In your opinion, what are the greatest advantages and disadvantages of these activities? What advice would you give someone who was thinking about participating in extracurricular activities?

●● IMPROVISE ●●

CD 2 ◀))) **T.** **LISTENING** Adult education. Listen to this conversation between a radio talk-show
Track 50 host and a listener. Then answer the questions below.

1. What's Carla's criticism about higher education? Do you agree with her? Think of some
   examples that support her complaint, and some that show another side of the issue.
   Do you think this problem is getting easier or harder to overcome?

2. Why didn't Carla go to college? Would you say that this is a problem that affects
   women more than men in today's society? Explain your answer.

3. It seems that Carla already has a decent job. Why does she even want a college degree?

4. Why does the radio host apologize to Carla? Why might his next two suggestions be
   better than his first one?

5. Complete the following sentences to reflect what was said in the dialogue. Pay
   attention to whether you're making a prediction or a hypothesis.

   a. If Carla could take classes online, …
   b. If she got credit for her previous
      work experience, …
   c. If she finishes her degree, …

   d. If she could be 19 again, …
   e. When she looks online, …
   f. As more people take advantage of
      technology to do "distance learning," …

👥 **U.** Peer advisor You're meeting with a student from Senegal who will be studying at your
school next term. Explain some of the things students need to know and do in order to
succeed at your school. Give advice about choosing classes, the kinds of extracurricular
activities that are available, where to buy books, cheap places to eat in the neighborhood,
where to go for different kinds of advice and help, etc. The Senegalese student asks for
lots of advice and expresses anxiety. You tell him or her not to worry and offer to help.

👥 **V.** Guess what! You and a classmate have just gotten great internships, and you want to tell each
other all about them. Explain why you think you were chosen (what classes you had taken, who
wrote you letters of recommendation, etc.). Give each other advice about how to succeed in the
internship and how to use it to prepare for the next step in your education or job search.

W. Education is important … As a class, talk about the importance of getting an
education in today's world. Consider these questions:

1. What kinds of schools are best for what kinds of people?

2. What should people study?

3. What are some ways to pay for your education?

4. How many hours a week do you think you can work and still do well in your classes?

5. If extracurricular activities are available, do you think it's a good idea to participate in them?

6. What problems have you had relating to school, and how have you solved them?

7. What advice would you give to people who are planning the next step in their education?

INTERNET RESEARCH College life. Go to the website of a college or university
you're interested in. Where is it located? When was it founded and by whom? What
majors and degrees (BA, BS, etc.) are offered? Look at the catalogue, and find some
courses that interest you. What extracurricular activities are offered? Are there any you'd
like to join? Present this college information to your classmates.

6 A Class Discussion
"What do you mean by …?"

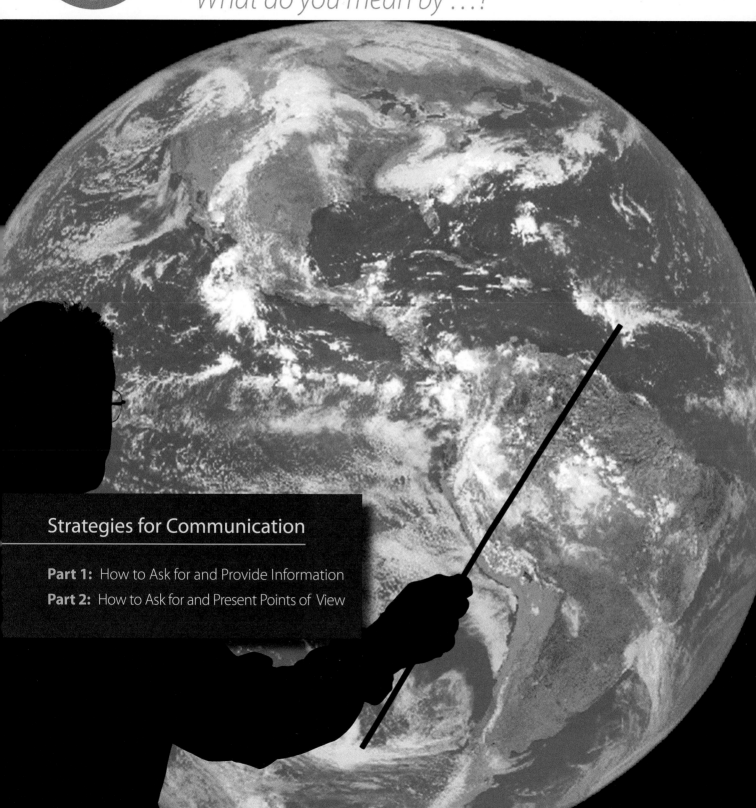

Strategies for Communication

Part 1: How to Ask for and Provide Information
Part 2: How to Ask for and Present Points of View

Part One

 **PREPARE**

A. PRE-LISTENING The five themes of human geography. Read the definitions of these five concepts used in the teaching of geography as they relate to the area of Southern California.

LOCATION refers to the various ways to indicate where something is situated. Location can either be absolute (referring to its placement on Earth by latitude and longitude) or relative (referring to its placement in relation to another location). For example, the latitude and longitude of Los Angeles is 34°3′8″N and 118°14′34″W. Los Angeles is north of San Diego.

PLACE is the description of the physical characteristics (deserts, rivers, lakes, mountains, etc.) and the human-created characteristics (buildings, roads, bridges, etc.) of an area. For example, most of southeastern California is desert. Freeways crisscross the state with major spaghetti-like interchanges in the large cities like Los Angeles.

HUMAN-ENVIRONMENT INTERACTION refers to how people depend on their environment, how they adapt to it, and how they change it. For example, a major part of California's economy is the wine industry. Those who make their livings growing grapes for wine have adapted their agricultural practices to the soils and climate of California. But because of the industrial development of the state, some cities like Los Angeles also have serious problems with air pollution.

MOVEMENT focuses on the reasons and ways that people, goods, and ideas travel from place to place. For example, Los Angeles is a very large and spread-out city, so people tend to use cars and public transportation to move around. Goods are transported by truck, ship, or airplane, while ideas travel by the media, communication, and the arts.

REGION refers to the shared characteristics that give a particular area its identity. These characteristics can be natural (e.g., climate, wildlife), physical (e.g., desert, Southern California, seaside), cultural (e.g., music, cooking, traditions), or human (e.g., professions, industry). For example, Southern California is a semi-tropical region with palm trees. Its history and location give the area cultural ties to Mexico (food, art, music, etc.).

Now match each item in this list with one of the five themes of human geography: **location, place, human-environment interaction, movement, and region**.

Desert: _____

Afro-Cuban jazz: _____

Immigrants: _____

The Panama Canal: _____

The White Earth Indian Reservation:

_____

A short train ride from here: _____

At the corner of Oak Street and Elm Street:

_____

The Internet: _____

Spanish-style architecture: _____

Emergency housing for hurricane victims:

_____

A flu epidemic: _____

GPS coordinates: _____

A rain forest: _____

A dam: _____

The Statue of Liberty: _____

Within walking distance: _____

Midtown Manhattan: _____

1600 Pennsylvania Avenue: _____

Road construction: _____

Made in China: _____

Birch tree forests and clear water lakes:

_____

Forest fires: _____

The Vine neighborhood: _____

A superstition: _____

Republic of Korea: _____

CD 3 🔊 Tracks 1–8 **B.** LISTENING Geography in the news. Listen to the excerpts from radio programs and check (✔) which of the five themes of geography they demonstrate. You may check more than one theme.

	LOCATION	PLACE	HUMAN-ENVIRONMENT INTERACTION	MOVEMENT	REGION
1.					
2.					
3.					
4.					
5.					
6.					
7.					
8.					

CD 3 ◀))) **C.** LISTENING I'm still confused about …   Listen to the conversation. Then, answer the
Track 9   questions that follow.

1. What question does the professor ask to get the discussion started?

_____

2. What is Quentin confused about?

_____

3. What questions does he ask to clarify his confusion? What expression does he use to
verify that he's understood?

_____

_____

_____

4. What examples of humans' effect on the environment are mentioned?

_____

_____

5. What question did Carla ask herself to make sure she understood the reading?

_____

6. What example did she come up with to answer her own question?

_____

_____

_____

Cultural Connections: Americans' Knowledge of Geography

Although students in the United States are well
prepared in many academic areas, their knowledge
of geography has traditionally lagged behind that of
students in other countries. This may be because the
United States is geographically isolated from much of
the rest of the world. As the individual nations have
become more connected though, U.S. schools have
given more emphasis to education in geography
and have developed creative ways to do so. Students
from grades 4 through 8 in U.S. schools (9- to 13-year-olds) are invited to participate in a
national geography competition that takes place every year in Washington, D.C.

How good is your knowledge of world geography? How much was geography emphasized
where you're from? Is it important to know about geography? Why or why not?

Anne: I don't think I did very well on that test. **What does** "relative location" **mean**, anyway? I must have been absent the day we talked about it. **Can you explain that** to me?

Alex: I think so. When we discussed it in class, **one example** that made sense to me **was** when we **applied it to** distance.

Anne: OK … **This** still **isn't clear to me**.

Alex: Hold on, I'm getting there. **How far** would you say we are **from** the beach right now?

Anne: **We're** really **close** to it! About three miles. If the traffic isn't bad, we could be there in ten minutes.

Alex: But what if you had to walk that distance twice a day, in 90-degree heat, carrying a jug of water on your head?

Anne: Gosh, **I see what you mean**. In that case, I guess three miles would seem really **far**.

Alex: That goes to show that everything is affected by **where** we live. **Where** we live **has a** big **impact** on **how** we live, on **what** we value, and on **how** we understand the world.

Anne: That's a really cool way of thinking about things …

PHRASES

Asking for Information

Who? / What? / When? / Where ?/ Why? / How?

What's the difference between [X] and [Y]?

What does [X] have to do with …?

How does [X] influence / affect [Y]?

Would(n't) / Could(n't) one / you say that …?

How would you describe / explain …?

What kind(s) of …?

What is the impact / effect / significance / meaning of …?

Can you / somebody explain [X] / give an example (of [X]), please?

How does [X] apply to …?

So does that mean …?

So you're saying that …? / So what you're saying is that …

Providing Information

You / One might say that …

Statistics / Studies show that …

Scientists believe that …

According to this map / our book / to the article by [X] / to what I found online …

I've read / heard / noticed …

I'm (pretty / quite / very) sure that …

If we look at (the case of) …, we can see that …

It appears that …

Scientists believe that …

Let me give (you) an example. / I've got an example.

Reacting to Information and Questions

I see what you mean.

That makes sense.

I'm not sure I agree / understand what you're asking.

That's a good question / example.

It's / That's (really) interesting / cool / amazing / confusing / awesome / strange (*etc.*)

I'm sorry, that (just / still) isn't clear to me.

I'm still confused about …

Could you repeat that / the question, please?

Note: See the *Speaker's Handbook* on page 165 for additional phrases.

Language Focus: *Less* and *Fewer*

In comparisons, **less** is used when referring to a singular noun.

> *I have **less** time than I used to.*
> *Studies show that there is about 11 percent **less** ice in the Arctic Sea each decade.*

Fewer is used in comparisons of plural nouns.

> *When the standard of living rises, people tend to have **fewer** children.*
> *Some studies claim there are **fewer** than 2000 giant pandas living in the wild today.*

D. Reading a map. Review the map below. Then, write six questions with phrases from the **Communicative Strategies** that can be answered using the map. Finally, write answers to your questions, followed each time by a reaction.

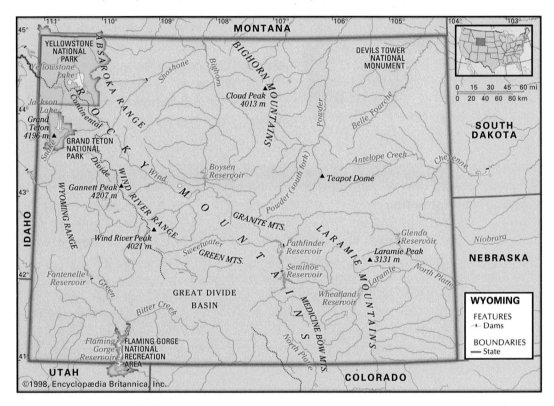

Example: Question: <u>How many mountain ranges are there in Wyoming?</u>

Answer & Reaction: <u>Looks like there are at least eight. That's amazing.</u>

1. Question: _____

Answer & Reaction: _____

2. Question: _____

Answer & Reaction: _____

3. Question: _____

Answer & Reaction: _____

4. Question: _____

Answer & Reaction: _____

5. Question: _____

    Answer & Reaction: _____

6. Question: _____

    Answer & Reaction: _____

E. I need to do some research. You've been offered a job in a part of the world you know nothing about. Using phrases from the **Communicative Strategies**, write six questions and your reasons for asking them in order to get information about the area before responding to the job offer.

    Example: What's the air quality like? I've read that there's serious air pollution in [name of place] and I have asthma.

Name of country, region, or city: _____

1. _____

2. _____

3. _____

4. _____

5. _____

6. _____

F. Here's how I'd describe it … Describe the place you are originally from, the place you now live, or another place you know well. Use phrases from the **Communicative Strategies** to write at least two informational sentences relating to each of the five themes of geography.

    1. Location

    _____

    _____

    2. Place

    _____

    _____

    3. Human-Environment Interaction

    _____

    _____

    4. Movement

    _____

    _____

    5. Region

    _____

    _____

TALK

G. **The five themes of human geography.** As a class, talk about how you classified the items in Activity A. Give additional examples to illustrate each of the five themes.

H. **Peer correction.** With your classmates, compare your answers to Activity D. Make corrections and additions to your answers as necessary.

I. **I need to do some research.** Compare the questions you wrote for Activity E with those of your classmates and make any necessary corrections. Then, discuss why the questions you asked are of particular importance to you.

J. **Here's how I'd describe it …** Working with a classmate, tell each other about the places you described in Activity F. Compare the places you described. Using phrases from the **Communicative Strategies**, give appropriate reactions to the information your classmate presents, ask follow-up questions, and keep the conversation going.

K. **Brainstorming.** With your classmates, discuss how you might divide your state (province, country, etc.) into regions. Describe how some of the regions might look different from the one you live in, and discuss how people's lives might be affected by those differences.

> **Example:** **A:** *Well, first of all there's the southern part of the state. It's really different from everything else.*
> **B:** *How is it different?*
> **A:** *Well, it's very rural. It's mostly agricultural.*
> **C:** *That makes sense. But so what?*
> **A:** *Well, people there live differently from the way we live in the north.*

L. **Discussion.** Discuss the following question with your classmates: Why is it important and useful to look at the world through the five themes of human geography?

Part Two

●● PREPARE ●●

LISTENING COMPREHENSION: *Taking Notes*

Taking good notes in a college lecture is a skill that improves with practice. Here are some techniques for getting the most important information down on paper, so you can reread and study it later.

- Listen for the ways your professor draws your attention to important points. These can include using particular phrases ("The main principles of this theory are …," "Essential to your understanding of this topic is …"), repeating an idea, or spelling a particular word or writing it on the board. Develop a way to highlight these points in your notes (underlining, adding asterisks or exclamation points, etc.).
- Listen to words that tell you how the lecture is structured. ("First," "Next," "Another approach that can be applied to this problem is…") You can then add words like: "*3 principles #1, #2, #3*" to your notes to help you prioritize and organize the information you've written down.
- Find brief ways to write down the main points of long sentences. This could mean writing only the subject, verb, and direct object, or a few important words in the sentence. Find ways to abbreviate some of the words you use. "*maj. prob. w/theory – diff. labs get diff. results (ex. Los Alamos lab experiment).*"
- If you miss something, write down enough that you can ask a question later, and put a star or other symbol in the margin to help you locate the problem. (**large failure rate ???? % **maj. cause = ???)

CD 3 Tracks 10–15 **M.** LISTENING Fill in the gaps. Listen to the short excerpts related to geography and fill in the blanks. Use the strategies in the **Listening Comprehension** to take your notes (abbreviations, question marks, etc.).

Example: You hear:

Scientists are convinced that the severity of the damage caused by Hurricane Katrina in New Orleans, Louisiana, was a direct result of the destruction of wetlands. The levees built to keep high water in the rivers from flooding the city were poorly constructed and broke in at least 20 locations as a result of the storm.

You write:

Scientists are convinced that the severity of the <u>dam. caused / Hurr. Katrina</u> in <u>N Orl, LA</u>, was a direct result of the <u>destr. wetlands</u>. The levees built to keep <u>hi wat in riv fr flooding city</u> were poorly constructed, and broke in at least <u>20 loc.</u> as a result of the storm.

1. Medford, _____, is just _____, but because it lies on the other side of the _____, it takes more than _____ to drive there. The best way to get there is to go _____, and then to turn _____ to reach the _____.

2. Minneapolis and _____ are called the _____,
but people often refer to _____ simply as "Minneapolis." This
_____, as they resent having their identity "swallowed up" by the
name of their _____.

3. _____ often train in _____ cities like
_____. Because there's about _____ at an altitude of
_____ above sea level, athletes produce more _____,
and thus their _____.

4. _____ has created new ways for people to become victims of
_____. When posting photos taken by _____,
you may be broadcasting your _____ to anyone with even a
_____. You should always _____ that transmits this
"metadata" about your location _____.

5. A recent _____ proposes to block any _____,
for fear that invasive fish species like the _____ might take over
the _____. The carp are gradually making their way up the
_____. If they were to populate _____,
this would eventually choke off other fish, because the carp would consume
_____.

6. In the past, _____ by pouring them down the drain or
flushing them down the toilet. But _____, so they ended up in
_____. This can harm all _____.
Nowadays, _____ have programs that take care of this. If you
_____, they'll dispose of them safely.

CD 3))) **N.** LISTENING On your own. Take notes about the main points and some of the details
Tracks
16–19 of the excerpts from geography lectures. Try to organize your ideas so that you'd be
able to understand them later. Use your own abbreviations, and use question marks to
indicate things you might want to ask about.

1. _____

_____

_____

_____

_____

2. _____

_____

_____

_____

_____

_____

3. _____

_____

_____

_____

_____

_____

4. _____

_____

_____

_____

_____

_____

_____

COMMUNICATIVE STRATEGIES: *How to Ask for and Present Points of View*

Kim: My mom is always getting upset when I post photos of myself while I'm still at the place where I'm taking the pictures. She doesn't think it's safe. **What do you** guys **think about that?**

Jeff: **I think** she should lighten up about that – everybody does it.

Javier: Sorry, but **I disagree. In my opinion, it could be** dangerous.

Kim: Really? **Don't you think** she's being a little bit overprotective?

Javier: **I'm not so sure.** Even if it's not very likely that someone would try to follow you or something, **it is possible** … Why take the chance?

Jeff: You know what? I guess **you're right**. It wouldn't hurt just to wait 'til you get home to do it.

PHRASES

Asking for and Giving Opinions
What do you think (about …)?
What's your opinion (about …)?
Do / Don't you (really) think that …?
Do you have any ideas / What are your ideas (about …)?
Do you agree (that … / about … / with …)?
I think / believe / am quite sure that …
In my opinion / view …
The way I see it, …
I'd say that …

Agreeing and Disagreeing
Exactly! / Absolutely (not)! / Definitely (not)!
I (definitely) agree / (completely) disagree (with…)
I suppose / I think / I'm sure you're right.
Not necessarily.
I don't agree (with …)
I don't think so.
Well, I'm not so sure about that.

Hypothesizing
I suppose / imagine that …
I wonder whether …
It might / could be that …
If that's true, then …
Do you think it's because …?
I'm guessing that …
Maybe it's because …
It's possible (that …)

Note: See the *Speaker's Handbook* on page 165 for additional phrases.

O. **Do you agree?** Read the general topic, and then state an opinion you have about a specific part of that topic. Then, write a response to the opinion as if you were someone else. Use phrases from the **Communicative Strategies** for expressing opinions, agreeing, and disagreeing.

Example: Global warming

Opinion: I think that the taxes on gas and oil should be really high because the use of those fuels contributes to global warming.

Response: I completely disagree! If we did that, the economy would collapse!

1. Global warming

Opinion: _____

Response: _____

2. Urban sprawl (the expansion of cities)

Opinion: _____

Response: _____

3. Recycling

Opinion: _____

Response: _____

4. Wildlife conservation

Opinion: _____

Response: _____

5. Population growth

Opinion: _____

Response: _____

P. Maybe it's because …   Write two hypotheses that might explain each statement. Use a variety of phrases from the **Communicative Strategies** and other phrases you know to express your theories.

1. People who move to the desert in the American Southwest often try to have the same kinds of green lawns they had in cooler climates.

a: _____

b: _____

2. Some people think it's a huge problem that so many try to climb Mount Everest each year.

a: _____

b: _____

3. Some French Canadians want to make the province of Québec a separate country from Canada.

a: _____

b: _____

4. In the early 20th century, new immigrants to the United States wanted their children to learn English as quickly as possible.

a: _____

b: _____

5. The railway system in the United States is underdeveloped and in disrepair—especially compared to Europe and Asia.

a: _____

b: _____

Q. Eating local. Some people believe that, for environmental reasons, we should not eat or drink anything that is imported from outside the area in which we live. In the space below, write notes in response to the questions. You will discuss this topic with your classmates later.

Hypothesis / Hypotheses:

What environmental benefits might result from eating local?

_____

_____

_____

What products would be easy to produce locally in the geographic area where you live?

_____

_____

_____

Which products would be difficult or impossible to produce? Where do your local markets currently get those products?

_____

_____

_____

Would you agree to try this approach to eating? Why or why not? What things would be hard for you to give up?

_____

_____

_____

 **TALK**

R. Peer correction. With your classmates, compare your answers to Activity O. Make corrections and additions to your answers as necessary.

S. Maybe it's because ... With a classmate, compare the answers you wrote for Activity P, making any necessary corrections to your answers. Then, respond to each other's hypotheses. Do you agree with them?

T. Eating local. With a group of classmates, discuss the idea of only eating and drinking things produced in your immediate area. Is this a good idea? Would you try it? How would you have to do things differently? In your discussion, use the notes you took in Activity Q.

U. Faster than ever. In the modern world, ideas move much faster than they did in the past. What technologies have made this possible? How would your life be different if you didn't have much information about the rest of the world? How has the rapid movement of knowledge and information changed our ways of life? Which changes do you consider positive and which negative? Discuss these questions with your class.

Professional Context: The Challenges of Living and Working Abroad

Sometimes corporations need to relocate employees and their families to other countries or regions of the world. In the past, families might have trouble adjusting to new cultures, resulting in their returning home early, which was disruptive and costly for everyone.

Today, many companies have orientation programs for employees and their families to prepare them for living in a new culture. They also provide on-site support as their employees adjust to new assignments, help with housing, transportation, and school for children. Local contacts employed by these companies may act as resources for problems that may arise in daily life. This approach has increased the success rate of overseas assignments and has benefitted both employers and employees.

CD 3 🔊 **V.** LISTENING **The rural exodus.** Take notes while you listen to this excerpt from a
Track 20 geography lecture.

1. As a class, create a summary of the lecture. Ask each other questions to fill in any gaps in understanding you might have.

2. Discuss the concept of the rural exodus. Compare the situation in Africa and the particular case of Kibera to other situations you might know about. Hypothesize about what possible causes and solutions experts might be considering.

3. Imagine that you're journalists preparing to write a story about the Kibera slum by interviewing someone who lives there. As a class, make a list of respectful questions you could ask so that your story would truly represent that individual's point of view. Include questions suggested by the lecture you just heard, and questions to find out what your interviewee might see as possible / partial solutions to some of the challenges posed by life in Kibera.

W. We all came from somewhere. With your classmates, discuss what you know about the population of the city in which you live.

  1. Who were the people who first lived there?

  2. What other groups moved in afterward? What ethnicities do they represent?

  3. Where did they come from? Why did they come?

  4. Do they live together in certain areas of the city, or are they scattered throughout?

  5. Are they completely integrated into the population, or do they still maintain separate cultures?

  6. Have their identities affected the character of your city (e.g., in street names, architectural styles, new kinds of foods or music, etc.)?

  7. Do generations of families hold the same types of jobs, or are younger people free to explore other careers?

  8. Do you know people who have moved away from your city? Where did they go and why?

X. The globalization of culture. With your classmates, discuss how popular culture is composed of elements and influences from other cultures. If possible, bring an example to class to share with your classmates. Possible aspects of culture to discuss: music, food, sports, clothing, games (including video games), films, animated films, literature (including manga), art, and advertising.

Y. Where we live. You've seen many examples of how the world can be described through the five themes of geography. As a class, use those themes to give a multi-dimensional portrait of the place where you live. What is its exact location? What are its natural characteristics and the physical changes made by humans? In what ways does the environment affect the humans who live there? How do people, goods, and ideas move around? What are its regional identities?

INTERNET RESEARCH A virtual tour. Select a region or country in the world that you'd like to learn more about. Then, using the five themes of human geography as your guide, go online and find out as much as you can about that region or country. Be prepared to talk to your classmates about it.

7 On the Job Market

"I got an interview!"

Strategies for Communication

Part 1: How to Exchange Information

Part 2: How to Weigh Options and Make Decisions

 **PREPARE**

A. PRE-LISTENING This one looks interesting! Read the job advertisements from a local website. Then, answer the questions that follow.

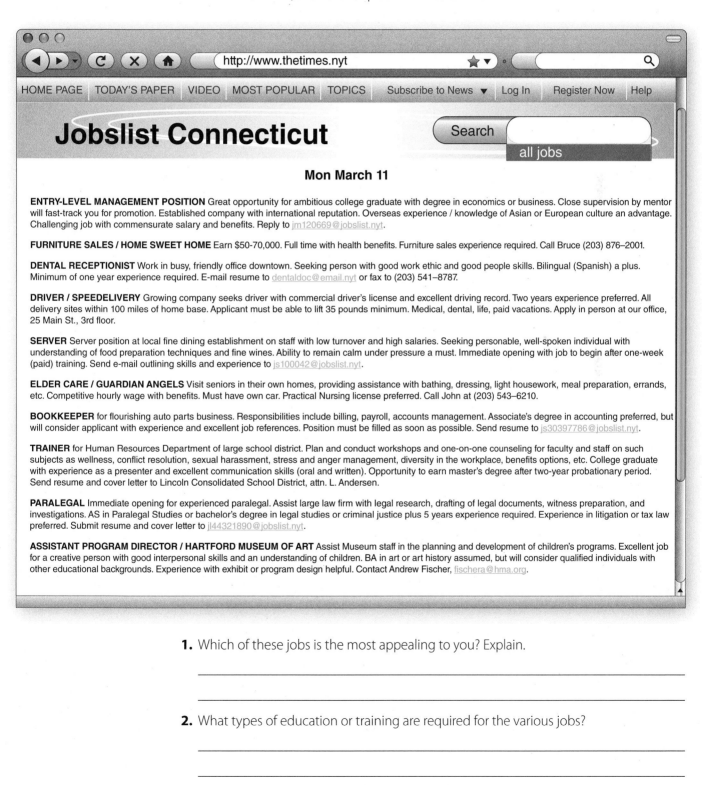

Jobslist Connecticut

Search all jobs

Mon March 11

ENTRY-LEVEL MANAGEMENT POSITION Great opportunity for ambitious college graduate with degree in economics or business. Close supervision by mentor will fast-track you for promotion. Established company with international reputation. Overseas experience / knowledge of Asian or European culture an advantage. Challenging job with commensurate salary and benefits. Reply to jm120669@jobslist.nyt.

FURNITURE SALES / HOME SWEET HOME Earn $50-70,000. Full time with health benefits. Furniture sales experience required. Call Bruce (203) 876–2001.

DENTAL RECEPTIONIST Work in busy, friendly office downtown. Seeking person with good work ethic and good people skills. Bilingual (Spanish) a plus. Minimum of one year experience required. E-mail resume to dentaldoc@email.nyt or fax to (203) 541–8787.

DRIVER / SPEEDELIVERY Growing company seeks driver with commercial driver's license and excellent driving record. Two years experience preferred. All delivery sites within 100 miles of home base. Applicant must be able to lift 35 pounds minimum. Medical, dental, life, paid vacations. Apply in person at our office, 25 Main St., 3rd floor.

SERVER Server position at local fine dining establishment on staff with low turnover and high salaries. Seeking personable, well-spoken individual with understanding of food preparation techniques and fine wines. Ability to remain calm under pressure a must. Immediate opening with job to begin after one-week (paid) training. Send e-mail outlining skills and experience to js100042@jobslist.nyt.

ELDER CARE / GUARDIAN ANGELS Visit seniors in their own homes, providing assistance with bathing, dressing, light housework, meal preparation, errands, etc. Competitive hourly wage with benefits. Must have own car. Practical Nursing license preferred. Call John at (203) 543–6210.

BOOKKEEPER for flourishing auto parts business. Responsibilities include billing, payroll, accounts management. Associate's degree in accounting preferred, but will consider applicant with experience and excellent job references. Position must be filled as soon as possible. Send resume to js30397786@jobslist.nyt.

TRAINER for Human Resources Department of large school district. Plan and conduct workshops and one-on-one counseling for faculty and staff on such subjects as wellness, conflict resolution, sexual harassment, stress and anger management, diversity in the workplace, benefits options, etc. College graduate with experience as a presenter and excellent communication skills (oral and written). Opportunity to earn master's degree after two-year probationary period. Send resume and cover letter to Lincoln Consolidated School District, attn. L. Andersen.

PARALEGAL Immediate opening for experienced paralegal. Assist large law firm with legal research, drafting of legal documents, witness preparation, and investigations. AS in Paralegal Studies or bachelor's degree in legal studies or criminal justice plus 5 years experience required. Experience in litigation or tax law preferred. Submit resume and cover letter to jl44321890@jobslist.nyt.

ASSISTANT PROGRAM DIRECTOR / HARTFORD MUSEUM OF ART Assist Museum staff in the planning and development of children's programs. Excellent job for a creative person with good interpersonal skills and an understanding of children. BA in art or art history assumed, but will consider qualified individuals with other educational backgrounds. Experience with exhibit or program design helpful. Contact Andrew Fischer, fischera@hma.org.

1. Which of these jobs is the most appealing to you? Explain.

2. What types of education or training are required for the various jobs?

3. Which jobs don't require applicants to have previous experience at all?

_____

_____

4. Which jobs mention the business that's hiring and which don't? Why do you think some businesses don't put their names in the job ad? If you don't know the name of the business, how do you contact it?

_____

_____

5. What are the various ways you can contact the companies to apply for a job?

_____

6. Which ads mention salaries? How specific are they? Why might some ads mention salary but others don't?

_____

_____

7. What kinds of extra knowledge or skills are mentioned in these ads that could give one candidate an advantage over others?

_____

_____

8. What language do certain ads use to suggest that the job they describe is difficult or intense?

_____

9. How do ads suggest that the applicant's personality will influence the hiring decision?

_____

10. Which job might allow you to continue your education with financial help from the employer?

_____

Cultural Connections: Benefits for U.S. Employees

As part of a job offer, an applicant must consider a company's _benefits package_ in addition to the salary. Benefits usually include health insurance, retirement, and vacation.

Most Americans don't have government-paid health care until they reach retirement age. Until then, they must subscribe to private health insurance, which is often arranged through their workplaces. Employers negotiate with an insurance company to cover their employees. Generally, the company pays part of the cost and the employee pays the rest. The amount the employer pays varies from job to job, and dental and vision coverage may or may not be included.

Companies often contribute money into retirement accounts for their employees. These accounts may be set up and paid into automatically, or companies may match money that employees contribute to their retirement fund.

Employers allow a certain number of paid vacation days. There is no set number of vacation days for workers. Employees may have one or two weeks of vacation per year when they first begin a new job.

As a general rule, employee benefits are only offered by employers to full-time (35-40 hours a week) employees.

How is health care provided where you come from: through a national health program, or private health insurance? What does the insurance cover? How much vacation do most people get?

CD 3 Tracks 21–27

B. LISTENING **You should apply!** Listen to the short conversations about the jobs advertised in Activity A and fill in the chart.

	JOB	IS THE PERSON QUALIFIED?	IS THE PERSON INTERESTED?
1.			
2.			
3.			
4.			
5.			
6.			
7.			

CD 3 Track 28

C. LISTENING **Career counseling.** Listen to the conversation. In the resume below, make the corrections the interviewer suggests.

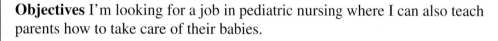

Janice Lee
Locust St., Chicago IL 60343, (312) 568–8262
vantard2@eclair.com

Objectives I'm looking for a job in pediatric nursing where I can also teach parents how to take care of their babies.

Education
Emancipation Community College, Aurora IL, 2012

Lincoln High School, Chicago IL, Graduated Spring 2009

Work Experience
Atrium Café, Chicago Health Clinic, 824 W. First St., Chicago IL
September 2011–August 2012
Server (served visitors, patients, doctors, and healthcare workers)

Chicago Health Clinic, 824 W. First St., Chicago IL June 2011–September 2011
Intern (did patient intake and assisted doctors with Well Baby visits and giving vaccination shots)

Chic Boutique, 425 Broad St., Elmhurst IL June 2009–September 2009
Sales Associate (assisted clients with purchases, worked cash register, handled customer complaints)

Skills
Basic nursing skills, some experience with pediatric nursing, fluent spoken Spanish

Human Resources rep:	I know this is a lot to absorb all at once. **Was there anything you didn't understand?**
Kent:	No, **I got most of it**, thanks. But **would you mind going over** that parental leave policy again?
HR rep:	No problem. You're eligible to take a leave after the birth or adoption of a child.
Kent:	Can you tell me **how much time** that is?
HR rep:	You'd get five weeks, with half pay.
Kent:	**Wait, you're saying that** fathers are eligible for this?
HR rep:	**Yes, that's the policy for fathers.** New moms get a bit more time.

PHRASES

Asking for Information and Clarification
Yes-No questions.
Who, what, when, where, why, how, *etc.*
What time, How many, How much, (For) How long,
    What kind of, Since when, Which …?
Is that [S-M-I-T-H]?
I'm not sure what you mean by…
Do / Did you mean … (or …)?
So, you're saying that …
You don't mean …, (do you)?
Could you be more specific?

Giving Information and Clarifying Statements
Yes, that's correct / that's it.
Yes, that's exactly right.
Right. / Correct.
No, not exactly.
No, that's not quite right.
I meant to say (that) …
I (guess I) should have said …
To be more exact …
I probably didn't make myself clear.

Verifying Comprehension
Do you understand?
Do you see what I mean / what I'm getting at?
Did you get all of that?
Was that clear (enough)?
Does that make sense?
Did I understand (you) correctly?
Do you have any questions?

Signaling That One Has Or Hasn't Understood
Yes, I see / that's clear / I understand / I've got
    (most of) it, (thanks).
So sorry. I'm not sure I got it all.
Sorry, I'm not (quite) sure what you mean to say.
Would you mind explaining / going over … (again)?

Note: See the Speaker's Handbook on page 165 for additional phrases.

D. **Yes, that's right.** Complete these conversations with logical phrases for clarifying or for indicating whether or not something was understood. Use phrases from the **Communicative Strategies** and other appropriate phrases you know.

1. **A:** Your name is spelled S-M-I-T-H, I assume?

    B: _____ It's S-M-Y-T-H-E. Don't worry, it happens all the time.

2. **A:** We'd like you to work nights a couple of times a week.

    B: _____?

    A: Probably Wednesdays and Thursdays, if that works for you.

3. **A:** So I hope that gives you an idea of what your responsibilities would be.

    _____?

    B: Yes, I think everything is quite clear. If I come up with more questions, may I e-mail you later?

4. **A:** … so you see that this job is quite demanding. The salary is *commensurate* with the degree of difficulty, though.

    B: Um… _____. Does it mean that that the salary is higher because the job is difficult?

    A: Yes, _____

5. **A:** _____?

    B: Well, basic word processing, of course. And also spreadsheets. Web page software, too, if that's possible.

6. **A:** I thought you said you had experience working overseas.

    B: Oh, sorry. _____ that I *want to get* some experience working abroad.

7. **A:** _____?

    B: I just felt that I'd been there too long and it wasn't challenging enough. I'm looking for something that will push me a little more.

8. **A:** … so you see, I'm just really fascinated by business.

    B: What aspects of business? _____?

    A: Sure. It's market analysis and marketing that interest me the most.

An **infinitive** is the basic form of a verb. It always begins with the word **to** (*to read, to watch, to be*, etc.).
- It is most commonly used after a conjugated verb or a noun.
  I like **to read**.
  I wish I had more time **to read**.

A **gerund** is a verb form ending in **-ing**.
- Like infinitives, it can be used after a verb, and it can also be used as the subject of a sentence.
  I like **reading**.
  Reading is fun.
- When it is used with a noun, it generally comes before the noun, and it functions as an adjective.
  That is a **fascinating** story.
- It can also be used after a preposition.
  My little brother is really good **at reading**.

When describing a series of actions, use all infinitives or all gerunds; don't mix the two.
  I like **reading, swimming,** and **watching** movies.
  I like **to read, to swim,** and **to watch** movies.

E. Information, please! Write four questions you could ask to get information about each of the following subjects. Use a variety of phrases from the **Communicative Strategies** and other phrases you already know.

Example: to find out about someone's strengths and weaknesses
Do you consider yourself an organized person?

1. to find out about someone's educational background and current studies

a. _____

b. _____

c. _____

d. _____

2. to find out about someone's strengths and weaknesses

a. _____

b. _____

c. _____

d. _____

3. to find out about someone's interests and leisure time activities

a. _____

b. _____

c. _____

d. _____

F. My resume. Use the resume in Activity C as a model and fill out this resume with your own information. (You may invent the details if you prefer.)

Objectives

Education

Work Experience

Skills

●● TALK ●●

G. Peer correction. Compare your answers to Activities D and E with those of your classmates. Make corrections and additions to your answers as necessary.

H. According to your resume … Exchange the resume you wrote in Activity F with that of a classmate. Read what your classmate wrote and ask for more information, clarification, and examples. Discuss what kind of job(s) he or she is interested in.

I. What I care about the most. Choose the four factors from the list below that would be the most important to you in deciding on a particular job. Then, compare your list with that of a classmate. Ask each other for clarification about your choices. (*How high of a salary would you want? Would you refuse to work for a company that made a dangerous product?*). In what ways are you and your classmate similar? In what ways are you different?

Salary	Job prestige	Independence
Colleagues	(Geographic) Location	Job responsibilities
Commute time	Health benefits	Work schedule
Vacation time	Type of business	Work outdoors / at a desk

J. A good fit. Discuss the following question with a classmate.

1. What education, training, and experience do you think employers are looking for in job candidates?

2. What personality traits, social skills, and communication skills do you think employers find appealing?

Part Two

●● PREPARE ●●

LISTENING COMPREHENSION: *What to Do When You Don't Understand*

As non-native speakers of a language, you'll probably never understand everything people say to you. You don't actually need to understand everything you hear in order to participate in a conversation and respond appropriately. Here are some suggestions to keep yourself from getting too anxious when you miss a word here and there.

- Use the context of the situation to anticipate what people might say. (For example, what's the first thing a salesperson might say when approaching you in a store?)
- Listen for the main ideas, or for a specific piece of information you're looking for, and ignore details you don't really care about.
- "Let go" of unfamiliar words, and see whether you can understand the message without them. If one of those unknown words turns out to be important, you can ask about it later.
- Summarize what you think has been said to make sure you understand important details. (*So, if I've understood you correctly, there are three questions we need to consider...*). If you've misunderstood something, someone will probably correct you.

If all else fails, don't be afraid to admit that you don't understand, and ask for clarification. Most people will be gracious and glad to explain.

CD 3 🔊))
Tracks
29–33

K. Take a guess! The following five exchanges take place in a nice restaurant. The second speaker is having some trouble understanding the hostess and the server, so he uses a variety of approaches to figure out what's being said. Listen to the exchanges and answer the questions about each one.

1. Was the exchange …

successful? _____
unsuccessful? _____

2. Was the first exchange ("I'm Michelle …") …

successful? _____
unsuccessful? _____

Was the man's question about the menus necessary to maintain successful communication?

Probably necessary _____
Probably not necessary _____

3. The first part of this exchange was only partly successful. What went wrong?

_____

When the server repeats her question, the customer still doesn't understand the important word in the sentence. Should he ask to have it repeated again?

Yes. _____   No. Now he has another way to figure it out. _____

4. Was the first part of the exchange …

successful? _____   unsuccessful? _____

When the server says "Sorry," and repeats the question, was the communication …

successful? _____   unsuccessful? _____

5. Was the first exchange (about coffee) …

successful? _____   unsuccessful? _____

Was the second part of the exchange ultimately …

successful? _____   unsuccessful? _____

Why? _____

CD 3 🔊 **L.** LISTENING **You're hired!** Listen to the end of a conversation between the Human
Track 34   Resources representative of Guardian Angels Elder Care and a young woman who's just
been offered a job. Then, answer the questions that follow.

1. Mrs. Walker asks Ms. Sanchez a question that begins with "How long …?" How does
she answer and why?

_____

_____

2. Mrs. Walker gives a fairly long description of what Ms. Sanchez will be doing in this job,
and Ms. Sanchez doesn't understand all of it. How does she handle that?

_____

_____

3. When Mrs. Walker tells her what her salary will be, why doesn't Ms. Sanchez ask her to
repeat or explain what she said?

_____

_____

4. She does ask Mrs. Walker to repeat her request for her Social Security number, but only
after Mrs. Walker mentions it a second time. Why?

_____

_____

COMMUNICATIVE STRATEGIES: *How to Weigh Options and Make Decisions*

Eric: **Have you made up your mind about** where you're going to college?

Charlie: Yes. **It was a hard decision,** though. **On the one hand,** I've always wanted to live in New York. **On the other hand,** everything costs more in a city. So, **after a lot of thought**, I'm going to the smaller school.

Eric: But **if you got** a basketball scholarship, **couldn't you** go to New York?

Charlie: Maybe ... but **I'd** still **have to** borrow money. And **if I take out** too many loans, **it'll take** me forever to pay them off.

PHRASES

Weighing Options

I need to consider both / all of the
    possibilities (carefully).
On the one hand, ... (but) on the other ...
Although this [option], ... the other one ...
I know I would like ..., but ...
Here are the pros and cons of each choice ...
Each one has its advantages and
    disadvantages.
Either ... or ...

Making Decisions

(After giving it a lot of thought,) I've decided to / on ...
I'm going to take / go with ...
I think [this choice] is better for me / is right for me / is the
    best option for me.
[This choice] makes the most sense for me / to me.
I've (finally) made up my mind.
It was a hard / difficult decision / choice, but I'm going to ...
I've decided / I prefer (to) ...

Speaking Hypothetically

What if ...?
What would / might happen if ...?
What would you do / suggest?
If + [*simple past*], (then) + I / we would /
    could / should / might + *verb*
If + [*past perfect*], (then) I / we would have /
    could have / should have / might have +
    [*past participle*]
If I were you, ...
I / You / It might / could / should / ought to...
(Let's) suppose / say / assume / think about /
    imagine that ...

Talking about the Future

What will happen if / when ...?
What's going to happen if / when ...?
Who / What / When / Where / Why will ...?
It's possible / obvious / definite / evident / likely / certain
    (*etc.*) that ...
I'll / we'll, they'll (*etc.*) probably / definitely / never /
    always, *etc.*
[Maybe] He'll regret it. / [Maybe] He's going to fall.)
If + [*present tense*], (then) + [*future*] ... (If you're not careful,
    you'll have an accident.)
There's a good chance ...
There's not much chance ...
Someday / In 10 years / In / By 2050 / In the distant future ...

Note: See the Speaker's Handbook on page 165 for additional phrases.

M. In other words … For each of the phrases below, write two other ways of expressing the same idea. Use phrases from the **Communicative Strategies** or other phrases you know.

1. It would be good if you were more careful.

    a. _____

    b. _____

2. In the future, you'll probably be rich.

    a. _____

    b. _____

3. Just think! If you won the lottery …

    a. _____

    b. _____

4. This is what I plan to do.

    a. _____

    b. _____

5. Watch out! Otherwise, you may fall.

    a. _____

    b. _____

6. I wonder about the consequences of your making that decision.

    a. _____

    b. _____

Language Focus: The Comparative

For comparison of superiority,
    add **-er** to short adjectives
      My office is **smaller than** yours.
    add **-ier** to adjectives that end with a **-y**
      She's much **happier than** they are.
    use more with longer adjectives and with nouns
      The book is much **more interesting than** the movie.
      She has **more money than** I do, but I have **more friends.**

For comparisons of inferiority, use **less** with adjectives and singular nouns, and **fewer** with plural nouns.
• He's always been **less anxious** than his friends.
• In my last job, I earned **less money** and got **fewer benefits.**

For comparisons of equality,
    use **as +** *adjective* **+ as** or **not as +** *adjective* **+ as**
      My computer is just **as small as** yours, but it's **not as light.**
    use **as much** with singular nouns and **as many** with plural nouns:
      He has **as much time** as I have, but he doesn't have **as many projects as** I do.

Don't forget that the comparative forms of **good** and **bad** are irregular.
• He's **good,** but she's a **better** writer **than** he is.
• The first movie was **bad,** but the sequel was **worse than** the original.

N. Decisions, decisions ...   Write one or two sentences mentioning the pros and cons of each choice listed below. Then, write a sentence saying what you would decide in each case and why. Use phrases from the **Communicative Strategies**, or other appropriate expressions.

Example: Bringing your lunch to work or eating out

Pros and cons: Although you save money by bringing your lunch, you can socialize with your coworkers if you go out.

Your decision: I would prefer to go out for lunch. I don't have time to make my lunch in the morning.

1. living alone or living with family members

Pros and cons: _____

Your decision: _____

2. buying a car or taking public transportation

Pros and cons: _____

Your decision: _____

3. calling friends or texting them

Pros and cons: _____

Your decision: _____

4. going for a run or going swimming

Pros and cons: _____

Your decision: _____

5. eating fast food or making a salad for yourself

Pros and cons: _____

Your decision: _____

Cultural Connections: Part-Time Jobs for Kids

Parents in the United States sometimes encourage their children to get a part-time job, even at a rather young age, to teach them a sense of responsibility. Their first jobs may include babysitting, delivering newspapers, mowing lawns, or walking a neighbor's dog. For American kids, taking on the responsibilities of a job is often considered a first step in achieving independence from their families. With the money they earn, children might choose to buy some of their own clothing or pay for their own entertainment (music, movie tickets, etc.). But parents usually encourage them to put some of their earnings in the bank to begin practicing financial responsibility.

When do people generally get their first jobs where you're from? What reasons motivate them to work? What kinds of jobs do they do? What do they do with the money they earn?

O. Help wanted. Read the job description below.

- Make a list of five questions you would ask a candidate if you were interviewing him or her for the job. Include at least one hypothetical question to find out what the candidate would do if faced with some obstacle or challenge.
- Then, make a list of five questions you would ask the interviewer if you were applying for the job. Include at least one question about what kind of future you might expect if you worked for this employer.

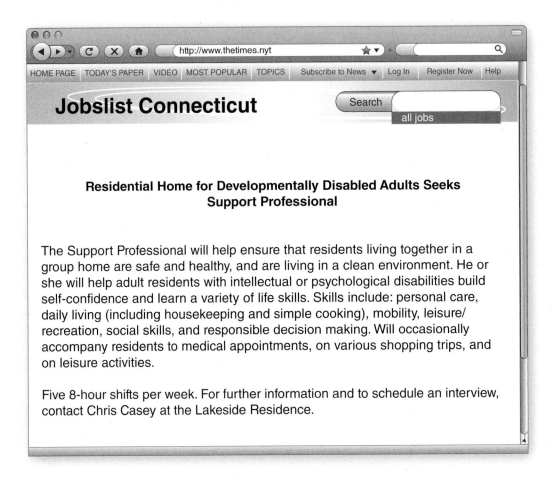

http://www.thetimes.nyt

HOME PAGE | TODAY'S PAPER | VIDEO | MOST POPULAR | TOPICS | Subscribe to News ▼ | Log In | Register Now | Help

Jobslist Connecticut

Search | all jobs

Residential Home for Developmentally Disabled Adults Seeks Support Professional

The Support Professional will help ensure that residents living together in a group home are safe and healthy, and are living in a clean environment. He or she will help adult residents with intellectual or psychological disabilities build self-confidence and learn a variety of life skills. Skills include: personal care, daily living (including housekeeping and simple cooking), mobility, leisure/recreation, social skills, and responsible decision making. Will occasionally accompany residents to medical appointments, on various shopping trips, and on leisure activities.

Five 8-hour shifts per week. For further information and to schedule an interview, contact Chris Casey at the Lakeside Residence.

Questions for Candidate

_____

_____

_____

_____

_____

Questions for Interviewer

_____

_____

_____

_____

_____

TALK

P. **Peer correction.** Compare your answers to Activities M and N with those of your classmates. Make corrections and additions to your answers as necessary.

Q. **Role-play: Practice job interview.** Your instructor will give you and your partner a set of Activity Cards. Use the cards to role-play a job interview. Refer to the questions you wrote and the job description from Activity O. Use appropriate phrases you know, or phrases from the **Communicative Strategies**. When you're finished, switch roles.

Professional Context: What to Expect from Interviewers

In a job interview, the interviewer should explain clearly to you what the job responsibilities are, what the work environment is like, and what salary and benefits the employer offers.

Questions interviewers might ask you include: why you are interested in the job, what kind of work environment you prefer, how you work with colleagues, how your education and experience qualify you for the job, and how this job might fit into your overall career plans.

To prevent hiring discrimination, the United States forbids an interviewer to ask you certain personal questions such as how old you are, what your ethnic origins or religious beliefs are, or whether you are married or have children.

R. **Do's and don'ts for candidates.** With a classmate, think of as many things a candidate should do—and should not do—in order to have a successful interview. Discuss what might happen if the candidate does these things.

> **Example:** **A:** *You should be right on time or a few minutes early for your interview.*
> **B:** *I agree. If you're late, the interviewer will think you're irresponsible or that you're not really interested in the job.*

S. **The ideal boss.** With a classmate, invent the portrait of the ideal boss. What kind of personality is the most effective? What skills should he/she possess? What behavior do you like to see in interactions between bosses and workers? If you were a boss, what are some of the things you would and wouldn't do?

T. **Future plans.** With a classmate, discuss your plans for the future. What kinds of jobs are you considering? What academic preparations are you making for the career you'd most like to have? Are there any careers you've considered and then rejected? Which ones and why? Imagine yourself ten years from now and talk about where you hope to be living and what you hope to be doing?

 **IMPROVISE** 🗨️🗨️

CD 3
Track 35
🔊 **U.** LISTENING On the one hand … Fatima is in her senior year at a large U.S. university, and she has a decision to make. Listen to the conversation she has with her advisor. Then, answer the questions that follow.

1. What are the two options Fatima is considering right now?

2. What are the advantages and disadvantages of each one?

3. Fatima says she's been feeling anxious lately. Why might that be? Was she looking for jobs when this one came along?

4. What question does her advisor ask to help her decide which job she wants?

5. How does the advisor try to reassure her that she'll probably find a teaching job, if she wants one?

6. What might Fatima mean when she says that her life might be more complicated in a few years?

7. The advisor proposes a third option. What is it?

8. Which option does Fatima choose? What does she say about each job to convince herself that she's right?

9. Do you think Fatima made the right choice? If you were in her shoes, which of the three options would you choose?

👥 **V.** Interesting jobs. Tell your classmates about an interesting job that someone you know has. Explain what the job is, and what the person does. Explain why you think it's interesting, and whether or not you might be interested in doing the same work.

👥 **W.** On the job market. There are many things you need to do to prepare yourself for the job market. Discuss with your classmates how you decide what kinds of jobs are right for you, get the training you need, write a resume, locate job openings, apply for jobs, prepare for interviews, make a good impression, decide whether or not to accept a job, and negotiate a salary.

X. Jobs of the future. In your opinion, what kinds of jobs will have the most openings in the future? Why do you think so? If you were advising a friend about a job or career to think about, what would you recommend? Why?

 INTERNET RESEARCH Job ads. Go online and find several sites where jobs are posted. Find two different ads for jobs you might be interested in, and present the pros and cons of each one to your classmates.

8 The Neighborhood

"I'd describe it as pretty friendly…"

Strategies for Communication

Part 1: How to Talk about Where You Live

Part 2: How to Talk about Places and People

Part One

●● PREPARE ●●

A. PRE-LISTENING **Where do I belong?** A real estate agency published the following descriptions of three neighborhoods and one small town with homes for sale in each area. Read the descriptions and then answer the questions.

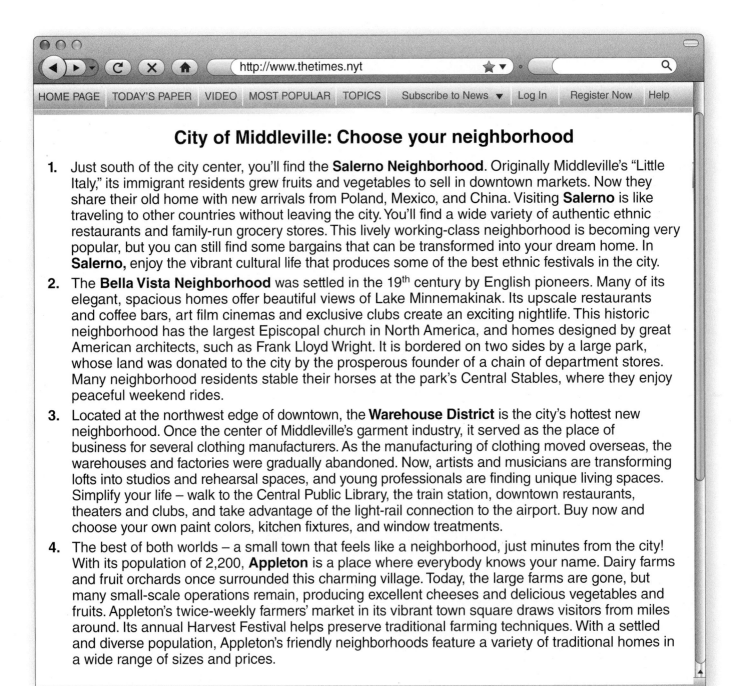

HOME PAGE   TODAY'S PAPER   VIDEO   MOST POPULAR   TOPICS   Subscribe to News ▼   Log In   Register Now   Help

City of Middleville: Choose your neighborhood

1. Just south of the city center, you'll find the **Salerno Neighborhood**. Originally Middleville's "Little Italy," its immigrant residents grew fruits and vegetables to sell in downtown markets. Now they share their old home with new arrivals from Poland, Mexico, and China. Visiting **Salerno** is like traveling to other countries without leaving the city. You'll find a wide variety of authentic ethnic restaurants and family-run grocery stores. This lively working-class neighborhood is becoming very popular, but you can still find some bargains that can be transformed into your dream home. In **Salerno,** enjoy the vibrant cultural life that produces some of the best ethnic festivals in the city.

2. The **Bella Vista Neighborhood** was settled in the 19th century by English pioneers. Many of its elegant, spacious homes offer beautiful views of Lake Minnemakinak. Its upscale restaurants and coffee bars, art film cinemas and exclusive clubs create an exciting nightlife. This historic neighborhood has the largest Episcopal church in North America, and homes designed by great American architects, such as Frank Lloyd Wright. It is bordered on two sides by a large park, whose land was donated to the city by the prosperous founder of a chain of department stores. Many neighborhood residents stable their horses at the park's Central Stables, where they enjoy peaceful weekend rides.

3. Located at the northwest edge of downtown, the **Warehouse District** is the city's hottest new neighborhood. Once the center of Middleville's garment industry, it served as the place of business for several clothing manufacturers. As the manufacturing of clothing moved overseas, the warehouses and factories were gradually abandoned. Now, artists and musicians are transforming lofts into studios and rehearsal spaces, and young professionals are finding unique living spaces. Simplify your life – walk to the Central Public Library, the train station, downtown restaurants, theaters and clubs, and take advantage of the light-rail connection to the airport. Buy now and choose your own paint colors, kitchen fixtures, and window treatments.

4. The best of both worlds – a small town that feels like a neighborhood, just minutes from the city! With its population of 2,200, **Appleton** is a place where everybody knows your name. Dairy farms and fruit orchards once surrounded this charming village. Today, the large farms are gone, but many small-scale operations remain, producing excellent cheeses and delicious vegetables and fruits. Appleton's twice-weekly farmers' market in its vibrant town square draws visitors from miles around. Its annual Harvest Festival helps preserve traditional farming techniques. With a settled and diverse population, Appleton's friendly neighborhoods feature a variety of traditional homes in a wide range of sizes and prices.

1. In your opinion, what kinds of people are likely to be attracted to each of these neighborhoods?

Salerno: _____

Bella Vista: _____

Warehouse District: _____

Appleton: _____

2. Which neighborhood appeals to you the most? Explain.

_____

3. Why does each description give information about the neighborhood's history?

_____

4. What gives each of these areas its unique identity?

_____

_____

5. How would you define the word *neighborhood*?

_____

_____

_____

CD 3 🔊
Tracks
36–43

B. LISTENING Every place is unique. Listen to the statements. Then fill in the chart, noting whether the speaker is talking about the past or the present, what adjectives are used to describe places, and what specific places are mentioned.

	PAST OR PRESENT?	ADJECTIVES	PLACES MENTIONED
1.			
2.			
3.			
4.			
5.			
6.			
7.			
8.			

C. LISTENING Welcome to the neighborhood! Listen to the conversation. Then answer the questions.

1. Why have the Leslies moved to Minneapolis? Were they unhappy about moving?

_____

2. What four types of people have lived in this neighborhood over the years?

_____

3. Bill was an art director in California. Name two or three things he plans to do here.

_____

_____

_____

4. What's unusual about the neighborhood high school?

_____

5. What places in the neighborhood are mentioned in the conversation?

_____

6. Do the people who live in this neighborhood get along well? Explain your answer.

_____

Cultural Connections: Good Neighbors

In the United States, people from the same neighborhood often get together a couple of times a year for neighborhood parties (block parties), neighborhood watch meetings, or other reasons. Neighbors may organize projects like community gardens, recycling campaigns, and neighborhood cleanup. They may also help elderly people on their street with snow removal, small home repairs, or food shopping. And if strangers appear to be engaging in suspicious or criminal behavior, neighbors speak up.

There is a sense of solidarity among people who live on the same street. Even if neighbors aren't especially close friends, they may leave a house key with someone nearby. When they go away, they may ask the neighbor to collect the newspaper and mail, water plants, turn lights on and off, and call if something happens to the house while the owners are gone.

An unwritten code of trust and dependence between neighbors may be a carryover from the history of Americans' moving west, when they often left friends and family behind. This shared experience made it natural for them to take care of one another just as family and close friends would do.

What have the neighborhoods been like in the places you've lived? Have neighbors gathered for any reason? Why or why not? How well do you know the people who live in your neighborhood now?

COMMUNICATIVE STRATEGIES: *How to Talk about Where You Live*

Neighbor:	Hi, we're the Joneses. We're in that yellow house **across the street**. In case you haven't found the coffeemaker yet, we brought you some coffee and muffins…
New resident:	That's so nice of you. Wow, the muffins are still warm!
Neighbor:	Let me tell you a secret. **There's a** great **bakery within walking distance** of here.
New resident:	That's great. **We used to** live in the suburbs, and **we were always** in the car. **There weren't any stores** you could walk to.

PHRASES

Describing a Neighborhood

It's a(n) + *adjective* + neighborhood
You'll find it to be (very) + *adjective*
I'd describe it as + *adjective*

Sample adjectives

(sub)urban / safe / rough / quiet / noisy / friendly /
well-cared for / neglected / modest / upscale /
working-class / white-collar / close-knit / diverse /
ethnic / historic / run-down / etc.

What's in a neighborhood

There's a + *singular noun*
There are lots of (many / very few) + *plural noun*
There aren't any / (very) many + *plural noun*

Sample nouns

house / apartment building / park / school / shop or
store / library / coffee shop, green space / church /
synagogue / mosque / bakery / etc.

Who lives in the neighborhood

There are a lot of / few / many + *noun*
There are both + *noun* and + *noun*

Sample nouns

singles / couples / students / families / retired
people / elderly people / professionals / wealthy
people / middle-class people / working-class
people / lower-income people

Where things are located

That's down the street / at the end of the block /
    around the corner / next door / kitty corner
    [diagonally across] / about three blocks from here
It's within walking distance.
You can ride your bike.
It's too far to walk. You'll have to take your car.

Indicating that you're talking about the present

There is / are …
We usually / always / sometimes / often / never /
    hardly ever, *etc.*
Now / These days / Since 1980 /
In the last few years, / Since the kids have been in
    school / Now that we're retired, …
They've just (built a new …)

Indicating that you're talking about the past

We used to …
There was / used to be …
We usually / always / sometimes / often / never / hardly
    ever, *etc.*
In the past, / 100 years ago / At the beginning, / In the
    middle, / Near the end of the 20th century, / Before
    I was born, / When my grandparents were young, /
    In 1984, *etc.*

Note: See the *Speaker's Handbook* on page 165 for additional phrases.

D. Survey. Complete the following short survey. Use phrases from the **Communicative Strategies** and any other appropriate phrases you know.

    1. If you could have exactly four places (businesses, shops, schools, etc.) within walking distance of where you live, which places would you choose?

    _____

    2. What are four adjectives that would describe your ideal neighborhood?

    _____

    3. Name four adjectives that describe a neighborhood you wouldn't care to live in.

    _____

    4. Name four kinds of people you'd enjoy having as neighbors.

    _____

Language Focus: The Present and Past Progressive

The **present progressive** (or present continuous) tense is used to describe things that are in progress right now or that are going on during a particular time period.

    Could you wait a few minutes? **I'm talking** with the real estate agent **right now**. What a drag! **We're moving** again!

Similarly, the **past progressive** tense is used to describe things that were happening at a particular moment or in a particular time period in the past.

    She **was still packing** when the movers arrived.
    We **were still living** there when my father died.

To form these tenses, use the present or past forms of the verb **to be**, and then add **-ing** to the main verb.

E. Riddles. Write riddles like the ones in the examples. Use phrases from the **Communicative Strategies** and any other appropriate phrases you know. Remember to include the answers.

    1. Describe three neighborhoods so that a classmate can guess who lives there.

        Example: There are lots of small houses. It's very quiet, and the lights go out at about 9:30 at night. Sometimes, there are young children there on the weekends, but not during the week. (Answer: elderly people)

        a. _____

        _____

        b. _____

        _____

        c. _____

        _____

2. Describe the location of three places on your campus or in your town. Your classmates will guess what it is.

Example: <u>It's too far to walk. It's downtown, about two blocks from the movie theater, right</u>
<u>next to the bookstore. (Answer: the Chinese restaurant)</u>

a. _____

_____

b. _____

_____

c. _____

_____

F. **Then and now: Describing your neighborhood.** Think of a neighborhood—yours, one you know, or one you invent. Write some notes on how it used to be, what has changed, and how it is now. Use a variety of phrases from the **Communicative Strategies** and other phrases you already know.

Example:

i'd describe it as a working-class neighborhood.

There used to be…	*Later…*	*Nowadays…*
Italian immigrants	*new groups of immig.*	*peop. of Ital. / Irish descent*
kids used to walk to school	*school closed*	*kids take bus*

TALK

G. Peer correction. Compare your answers to Activity D with those of your classmates. Take note of which of your answers are similar and which ones are different.

H. Riddles. Read the riddles you wrote for Activity E to see whether your classmates can guess what kinds of people and what places you're describing.

I. Then and now. With a partner, and using the notes you wrote for Activity F, describe a neighborhood you know—both as it used to be and as it is now. Use phrases from the **Communicative Strategies,** ask each other follow-up questions, and keep the conversation going.

J. Not all neighborhoods are the same. With a classmate, look at the photos of the three different neighborhoods. Talk about how they resemble one another and in what ways they look different (inventing any details you wish). Use phrases from the **Communicative Strategies** and other phrases you know, and keep the conversation going.

1. 2. 3.

K. What I care about most. With a classmate, talk about the factors that would be the most important to you in choosing a neighborhood to live in, and why. In addition, imagine what kind of neighborhood you would want if your circumstances were different (such as if you were older or younger, had children or not, were married or single, etc.).

Example: *I wouldn't care much about access to public transportation because I've got a car. But if I were older and didn't want to drive anymore, I'd want to be near a bus line.*

Useful Vocabulary

quality of the schools	nightlife	access to public transportation
noise level	shopping	trees, green spaces
safety	friendliness	access to healthcare
diversity	architecture	age of neighborhood
prestige of neighborhood	access to culture	appearance

 **PREPARE**

LISTENING COMPREHENSION: *Making Inferences*

If you listen carefully to people you can often make an **inference** (draw a conclusion) about what they mean to say. In order to arrive at logical conclusions about what might be implied by what people say, you will need to …

- ***listen for clues in what they say—or don't say.*** For instance, if a mother says, "My older son is always very neat," you might infer that she has a younger son who is not neat. Or, someone who says, "She wants you to think she's got a great job" is giving a very strong hint that that's not the case.

- ***consider your own knowledge about how people behave and talk.*** For example, you know that when people get upset talking about an unfortunate situation, it's often because they've had a similar experience. Or, if friends hesitate to give an opinion about your paper, you might suspect that they don't think it's very good. People often behave like that when they don't want to hurt someone's feelings.

- ***draw on similar experiences from your own life.*** Let's say you hate going to big parties where you don't know anyone. If your friend says he's going to a party like that, you might automatically listen for clues to see whether you can tell how he feels about it.

Try to listen in an "arc," or overall message, and not just to individual words and sentences. If you do, you'll often find that a piece of information you hear later explains something you heard earlier.

After making a reasonable inference, keep listening for other aspects of the conversation that support or reject your conclusion.

CD 3
Tracks
45–52

L. LISTENING I suspect that … Listen to the short conversations. Then answer the questions by making logical inferences.

1. What do you infer about the professor's opinion of this student? What makes you think so?

_____

_____

2. How does the man feel about his in-laws? How do you know?

_____

_____

3. How well do you think the girl knows Peter? Why do you think that?

_____

_____

4. What do you infer from what the speaker says about Alan? Do you think she wants the listener to make that inference?

_____

_____

5. Why might the man want to be assigned to the boss's group? What does he say that makes you think that?

_____

_____

6. Why do you think the woman is asking her friend for those names? How can you tell?

_____

_____

7. Why do you think the young man is asking the question he asks? What makes you think so?

_____

_____

8. What do you infer from the odd request the professor makes of the job candidate? What supports your interpretation?

_____

_____

CD 3 🔊
Track 53

M. LISTENING Reading between the lines. Listen to the conversation. Then answer the questions that follow.

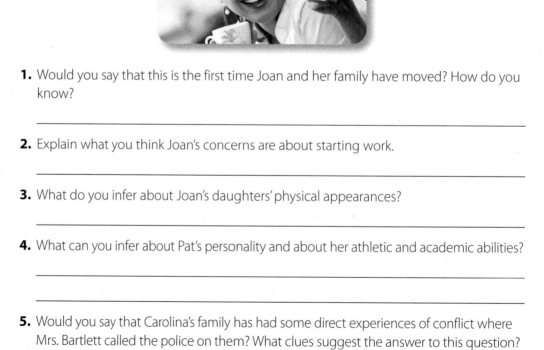

1. Would you say that this is the first time Joan and her family have moved? How do you know?

_____

2. Explain what you think Joan's concerns are about starting work.

_____

3. What do you infer about Joan's daughters' physical appearances?

_____

4. What can you infer about Pat's personality and about her athletic and academic abilities?

_____

_____

5. Would you say that Carolina's family has had some direct experiences of conflict where Mrs. Bartlett called the police on them? What clues suggest the answer to this question?

_____

Carol: Charlie, who's your dentist? I think I have a cavity.
Charlie: I go to Dr. Johnson. I don't deal well with pain and he's really gentle.
Carol: That's good. **I hate it when** they don't seem to care how you're feeling. **Where's his office?**
Charlie: **He's on White's Road. Go down** Oakland Drive **until you get to** White's. **Take a left,** and then an immediate **left** down that little hill. His office is at the far end of the parking lot.

PHRASES

Giving Directions

Can / Could you tell me where … is?
Can / Could you tell me how to get to … ?
Where is / Where's …?
(First) Turn right / left (at / onto Main Street)
(Next) Take a right / Take a left …
(Then) Go straight ahead (on Oak St. / Ave.)
Go down X St.
Go past / Cross / Go through the …
Drive / Walk two blocks / 200 yards / ½ mile, etc.
Keep going until you get to / see …
You'll see a (church / park, etc.) on your left / right.
It's the second street / house on the left, etc.
It's on Market Street.
It's on the corner of Porter St. and Davis Ave.
It'll be right across the street.

Talking about People

He's / She's / They're (very) …
I (dis)like it when people are …

Positive Character Traits

considerate, generous, enthusiastic, sincere, warm, friendly, affectionate, discreet, honest, supportive, funny, polite, loyal, open-minded, easygoing, calm, fair, patient, reliable, understanding

Negative Character Traits

bossy, interfering, pushy, nosy, arrogant, selfish, grouchy, hypocritical, superficial, snobbish, nasty, cold, standoffish, intolerant, stingy, cynical, dishonest, sneaky, self-centered, greedy, irresponsible, stubborn, rude, unreliable, conceited

Admiring / Appreciating

She'd do anything for you …
I have so much respect for …
I'm (very) grateful (to / for) …
I really appreciate / admire …
I appreciate it when …
I don't know what I'd do without …

Complaining

I hate / can't stand it when …
I'm really upset about …
It really bothers me when …
It makes me mad when …
I don't like the fact that …
She / He always / never …
That drives me crazy.

Note: See the *Speaker's Handbook* on page 165 for additional phrases.

N. **You can't miss it!** Think of a place in your town that's somewhat far away. Write directions for how to get from that place to the place where your English class is held. Be prepared to explain how to get there using at least two different means of transportation (on foot, by bike, driving a car, taking public transportation).

_____

_____

_____

_____

_____

_____

_____

_____

_____

_____

_____

_____

O. Highs and lows. For each of the situations below, write down one positive and one negative comment the first person might make about the other. Follow each comment with a specific example to support the criticism and the praise. Use a variety of adjectives and phrases from the **Communicative Strategies**, and other appropriate expressions.

Example: One spouse (husband or wife) talking about the other

My husband is really inconsiderate. When he gets up to get a snack while we're

watching TV, he doesn't ask me if I want anything.

Sometimes my husband is kind and generous. He's going to stay home with the kids

all weekend so I can go to Chicago and meet up with some high school girlfriends.

1. One spouse talking about the other

_____

_____

_____

2. One sibling (brother or sister) talking about a younger sibling

_____

_____

_____

3. One roommate / housemate talking about another

_____

_____

_____

4. One coworker talking about another

_____

_____

_____

5. An employee talking about the boss

_____

_____

_____

Professional Context: The Importance of Service in the Business World

Businesses involved in retail (selling goods directly to people) strive to give good service to the customers they interact with. Good service in business might include:

- Greeting customers with a smile.
- Asking customers if they need help and taking them to the right department.
- Helping customers find the right size, color, etc., of a product they're interested in and offering opinions about products.
- Helping customers find a solution if something isn't available.
- Calling regular customers about newly-arrived merchandise they might like and offering to hold it until they come to the store.
- Repairing certain items or exchanging them for new ones if they don't work properly.
- Accepting returned items and refunding the full purchase price if customers aren't satisfied.

An unspoken rule in American business has been "the customer is always right." This is especially true for small businesses. Local retail stores often can't sell merchandise at the same low prices as the larger chain stores (stores with multiple locations). One way they try to attract and retain loyal customers is by offering "service with a smile."

P. My neighbors. Prepare to talk about three neighbors you have now or had in the past. (Change their names if someone else might know them.) Try to choose neighbors who are very different from each other, and write notes on their personalities and the kinds of things they do. Use phrases from the **Communicative Strategies** or other appropriate expressions.

●● TALK ●●

Q. Peer correction. Compare your answers to Activities N and O with those of your class-mates. Make corrections and additions to your answers as necessary.

R. Have you got a pencil? Describe to a classmate how to get to where you live from some other place in your town. Your partner writes down the directions, asking you to repeat and clarify as needed, and then reads them back to you. You say whether the di-rections are accurate and make any necessary corrections. Then switch roles. Use phrases from the **Communicative Strategies** and other appropriate phrases you know.

S. Our neighbors. With a classmate, discuss the neighbors you described in Activity P. If you were making a television show about a neighborhood, which people you described would you include in your show?

T. I can't stand people who … With a classmate, discuss the kinds of personality traits you find the most disagreeable in other people. What kinds of traits and behaviors would make it impossible for you to be friends with another person?

U. My hero! You and a classmate each describe a person you admire. Describe what your person is like, and tell at least one story that shows the kinds of things this person does that make him or her admirable. Explain what this person has taught you, or what kind of influence he or she has had on your life.

 **IMPROVISE**

CD 3 ◀))) **V.** LISTENING Let's do lunch! Listen to the excerpt from a telephone conversation.
Track 54 Then answer the questions that follow.

1. Why is Andre living in Chicago? How do you know?

_____

2. Has Karl ever been to Chicago? How do you know?

_____

3. Where is Andre living, and what doesn't he like about it?

_____

4. What things does he appreciate about being there?

_____

5. Write down the directions Andre gives Karl to get from Chicago's main airport to the
hotel. Then write the directions from the hotel to the restaurant.

_____

_____

_____

_____

_____

W. A real character. Choose a character you find memorable from a book, a movie, or a
television show you know. Describe the character's positive and negative traits to a classmate, and explain why you find the character interesting. Your partner will also describe
a character. What do these two characters have in common, and how are they different?
How is each character's personality and behavior important to the stories they're part of?

X. Geographical concepts. Discuss a neighborhood you know well in terms of the
concepts of **place** and **human-environment interaction**, which you learned about in
Chapter 6. What are this neighborhood's physical features? What are the most significant
human-designed features? What does the presence—or absence—of certain human-
designed features reveal about the values of those who designed it? If you could change
this neighborhood in any way, what would you change?

Y. **A welcoming place?** With your classmates, discuss these questions. Does the American idea of "neighborhood" as a welcoming place where people support and look out for one another apply to the neighborhood or town where you live? If not, how would you describe the relationships between you and your neighbors? Do you all know one another? In what kinds of ways do you help one another? If you don't receive that sort of support from your neighbors, who does provide it? If you don't know your neighbors very well, would you like to know them better? Why or why not?

Z. **Things change.** In some neighborhoods of the modern United States, neighbors have far less face-to-face interaction with each other than in the past. With a classmate, discuss why this might be. Consider such factors as new technologies, changes in families and roles of family members, changes in the people who live in neighborhoods, and historical and sociological reasons.

Example: *I would guess that first-generation immigrants settled in the same neighborhoods and stuck together a lot because they didn't speak English very well. Their children and grandchildren spoke English, so when they grew up, they might've moved out of the neighborhood …*

INTERNET RESEARCH I never knew that! Go online and find information about the history of a well-known neighborhood in your town or about the place where your school is located. Share your findings with your classmates in order to get a better perspective on the places you know.

Activity B: Nice to meet you.

Professor M: Hello, I haven't met you before. I'm Professor Maciejewski, the instructor for this class. You can just call me Professor M., that's easier.

Hoshi: Thank you …, ah … Professor M. Yes, that's very much easier for me. My name is Hoshi Yamada.

Professor M: It's very nice to meet you, Miss Yamada. I usually call my students by their first names. Is that OK with you?

Hoshi: Yes, I'm very used to that.

Professor M: Where are you originally from, Hoshi?

Hoshi: My family and I moved here … from the region of Hyogo-ken in Japan. Um … from the city of Amagasaki.

Professor M: Is Amagasaki a large city?

Hoshi: I think it has almost … um … 800,000 people, fairly large for Japan.

Professor M: When did you arrive in the United States?

Hoshi: Three months ago. We came … moved here … because my father … how do you say … was transferred to his company in the United States.

Professor M: How long have you been studying English?

Hoshi: Ah … since I was 12. I took classes in school.

Professor M: Your English is very good, Hoshi.

Hoshi: Oh, it's not so good. I have to think very hard … uh … to find the right words.

Professor M: That's OK. In this class, you'll have many conversations with your classmates. That will help you feel more comfortable with English.

Hoshi: I hope so. I am taking another class this semester … I will work very hard to improve my English.

Professor M: What else are you taking?

Hoshi: Chemistry. I like chemistry. Maybe I could be a researcher when I finish my studies.

Professor M: That's very interesting. What kind of researcher?

Hoshi: Um … I think something in the field of medicine.

Professor M: Good choice! … Well … it's been nice talking to you, Hoshi.

Hoshi: Yes, Professor M. It was nice talking to you, too.

Professor M: OK, class, it's time to start. First, let's take attendance. Then you'll have the chance to introduce yourselves to each other.

Activity C: Let's introduce ourselves.

1

Hi. I'm … My name is Zahid. I am from the United Arab Emirates. I came to the United States … last summer … to ah … to study economics at the university. My wife … I came with my wife and two children. We are living with my uncle. He came here many years ago. My wife … she is studying … ah … psychology. Our children are in primary … elementary school. When we finish our studies … we are going back to the UAE.

2

Hi, everyone. I'm Mariana. I'm … how do you say … originally … from Brazil. But now my parents and … sister … and I live here. We are all learning English. But we speak Portuguese at home. I like … um … to have fun. I like sports very much, especially tennis and soccer. Someday I want to go to … medical school. So I can become a … so I can work in sports medicine.

3

Hello. I am … from China. Oh yes, my name is Li Ming. I came here to study English and to … ah … learn … to be a … teacher. Right now, I work as a volunteer tutor for children in a local school. When I return to China, I … ah … plan to be a teacher in a … an … elementary school. I very much like to work with young children. When I am not … When I have free time …, I like watching American movies. I also like to make drawings … I draw the things I see. I am starting an album … drawings … about the United States.

4

Hello, my name is Chul-Soo. I'm from Korea. Um … I came here to study computer science. But I very much need to practice my English. I am … um … ambitious. I want to return to Korea and get a position in an … international company. And I want to make much much money. In my free time, I play computer games. I think … here in the United States … I am called a "geek" … correct? But I like people also and want to make new friends.

Activity M: Professor M.

Amanda: So you and Carlos already took a course with … um … Professor M?

Ahmed: Yes. I … was in … I took … his other conversation course and Carlos also took the one last semester.

Mariko: So what is your … ah … opinion of Professor M?

Carlos: Hm … I think he's absolutely the best teacher.

Mariko: What's he like?

Ahmed: Well … he's very informal. He always wears jeans, a t-shirt or a sweater, and sneakers. He likes to laugh and … well … he's always in a good mood. I think he is a very positive person. We have a lot of fun in class.

Carlos: But, in my opinion, he is also very … um … strict. He does not like it if we don't do our homework. Like … he checks it at the beginning of each period. So make sure that you always do the work. He does not accept … excuses.

Ahmed: And, also, he expects us to participate in class. He wants us to try, even if we make mistakes … errors.

Amanda: But what is he like as a person?

Carlos: I believe he's very patient … and he never corrects us directly. When he hears a mistake, he brings it up … um … later and never points to the person who made the mistake. I like that. It means that I never get blamed when I'm wrong.

Ahmed: And, as far as I can see, he really believes that it's OK to make mistakes. He says that's how you learn.

Mariko: I'm not so sure. I don't like making mistakes and I get very … how do you say … embarrassed.

Carlos: I don't think you have to worry about that. You'll learn that Professor M is very interested in WHAT we say, not just HOW we say it. And he's very kind. He never embarrasses us.

Mariko: Does he ever teach us grammar, like verb tenses?

Carlos: Ah … only if he hears mistakes. Then he gives us a little lesson to remind us about the rules.

Amanda: Ahmed, what was all that stuff about a boat?

Ahmed: He's been building a boat like … forever. He's making it in his garage. He does everything by hand, like before there was electricity … no power tools.

Mariko: Have you seen it?

Carlos: Yeah. We went to his house at the end of the semester. It's not finished, but it's already beautiful. He seems to be very talented. Boats and boat-building are his hobbies. But he has many other interests, like sports … um … music … oh yeah, and the movies. He's a very … interesting … intelligent person. I'm absolutely convinced that's the reason he is such a good teacher.

Activity T: Phone conversations.

Conversation 1

Receptionist: Hello, Enterprise Auto. How can I help you?

Enrique: Good afternoon. My name is Enrique Fuentes. I'm calling about my car. I dropped it off this morning.

Receptionist: Yes, Mr. Fuentes. Let me connect you to the service department.

Enrique: Thank you.

Mike: Hi, this is Mike. What can I do for you?

Enrique: Yes, this is Enrique Fuentes. I'm calling about the car I dropped off this morning. The white one with the dent on the right side. I was told I could pick it up by two o'clock. It's now three, so I thought I would check in with you.

Mike: Actually, we were just going to call you. I'm afraid it won't be finished until tomorrow morning. The problem is more complicated than we thought. I think it can be ready by tomorrow between 11 and … let's say noon. It will cost about a hundred dollars more than the estimate. I need your approval before I can continue the work.

Enrique: Hm … I guess I don't have much choice. That's fine. Go ahead and do it. Can I be sure that you'll be done by 11 tomorrow?

Mike: Yes. But just to be sure, call us before you leave home.

Enrique: I'll do that. Thank you. Goodbye.

Mike: Goodbye, Mr. Fuentes.

Conversation 2

(phone rings)

Mother: Hi, honey, how're you doing?

Daughter: I'm going crazy, that's how I'm doing.

Mother: Why, what's going on?

Daughter: Where do I begin? First of all, I stayed home from work this morning because Jeremy isn't feeling well and I didn't send him to school. Eric has meetings all day, so he couldn't help.

Mother: Is Jeremy OK? Do you need to take him to the doctor?

Daughter: That's just it. I called the doctor and he thinks it's the flu. He wants to see Jeremy this afternoon. But I'm supposed to be on a phone meeting with a client at the same time. And then Suzie has to be picked up from school. And … Eric just called and he's not coming home for dinner. I just walked the dog, so she's OK for a while. And then …

Mother: Wait a minute … stop. You should've called me when everything started falling apart this morning. It's my day off, so here's what we're going to do. When's the doctor's appointment?

Daughter: It's at 3:30.

Mother: That's perfect. I'll pick up Suzie from Kindergarten at noon. Then we'll come to your house, I'll give Suzie a snack, and we'll take the dog for a walk in the park. Then we'll come back to the house to pick up Jeremy for the doctor's appointment while you're in the phone meeting. And then we'll all come back to the house and I'll either cook something or we'll order out.

Daughter: Really? You're a lifesaver. Thanks so much, Mom. I'm sorry to lay this all on you.

Mother: You know I don't mind. In my opinion, you need to stop being so stressed out. It's not healthy. When you need help, you should always just let me know.

Daughter: I would, normally. But I forgot that this was your day off.

Mother: It's OK. I'll go get Suzie now. Just relax. We all have days like this.

CHAPTER 1

Activity B: Preferences.

1

Samantha: So what do you think about this one? It says here that it's a watercolor.

Julia: It seems a bit … um … washed out to me. I prefer stronger colors. But I do like art that has a message … that says something. That's why this one actually appeals to me. The artist seems to have a real appreciation of nature. Yes, the more I look at it, the more it grows on me.

2

Matías: Our art teacher said we should write something about one abstract painting in this exhibit. What about this one?

Kristen: I'm not sure … I don't know what to think. I like how colorful it is … but I don't get it. I couldn't possibly talk about it because I don't get what the artist is trying to say. Maybe I just don't know enough about abstract art. I'm not particularly crazy about a painting that looks like a kid could have done it.

3

Sung-Jae: It says here that this bowl of apples and pears is a still life. I never know what to think about this kind of art. It's very realistic and I'm sure it's very difficult to paint fruit, but … I like art that tells a story.

Rick: I see what you mean. This isn't my favorite kind of art either.

4

Mary: Do you have any idea what the artist is trying to say in this painting?

Paul: Yes, I think the violence of the storm, with the dark clouds, the rain, and the heavy wind symbolizes the difficulty of life. See the two small figures trying to walk in the wind? They're struggling to move forward. It seems to me that this is the artist's idea of real life. This is awesome. I really like art that makes me think.

5

Mark: Hmm … what do you think? Is this the kind of art you like?

Tom: I know that the guy is famous … but I'm not really sure why. I usually like abstract art, but this is truly bizarre. There are shapes in there that I recognize, like the stop sign and the paperclip. And in the background there's a smartphone, I think … and a book here in the lower right-hand corner … The objects don't seem to be connected in any way. It does absolutely nothing for me.

6

Jennifer: This is kind of interesting. What do you think?

Maria: Well, it's certainly … ah … huge! It takes up the whole wall.

Jennifer: Yes, but what's your impression of it?

Maria: I know what you're asking! I just don't know how to answer. It looks really … how can I put this … really violent to me. Because of all the streaks and drops of red. It's mostly red with a little pink here and there. But I can't figure it out. I guess I would have to say that I don't dislike it and I don't like it. I can't make up my mind because I don't know what's going on in it. Maybe I just need to learn more about it.

Activity C: Special Exhibit: Laurence Young.

Guide: First, let me say a few words about Laurence Young that will help us understand his work. As a child he spent many hours exploring the woods, ponds, and waterways of his native Massachusetts … and that early experience later became the basis for many of his landscapes. When he moved to New York City as a young man, the drama of city life inspired him to start drawing the people and places he was experiencing. But, in the end, he settled in a small fishing village and returned to nature and to the feeling of safety of his childhood. Barns, boats, woods, sand dunes, people in peaceful settings, small town living – those became Young's images of choice in his work. They represent the quiet and solitude he seeks in his own life.

Pitched is one of Young's most well-known paintings. While he often uses a soft and muted palette, in this piece, the colors of the boat and its reflection are bright and intense. The reds and the well-placed splashes of white and yellow make it clearly stand out from the background. There seems to be an energy in the boat that suggests a sense of tension between being stranded at low tide and the desire for movement when the water returns. The boat's reflection in the water seems to tell us that the boat will be sailing again very soon.

In *Lattice Work*, Young uses the softer palette that characterizes many of his pieces: the patterns of color in the fence and the buildings, the blues of the water and the sky that almost blend together, the soft beige of the sand. Although the roofs are somewhat darker, they still don't have the brightness that we see in the boat. The background of the water helps to focus our attention on the fence and the buildings. But we don't see any details in the buildings. There might be a slight outline of a window, but the buildings are mostly patterns of color that make them look almost abandoned. Maybe that's why the painting is called *Lattice Work* – to focus more on patterns than on anything else.

These two paintings by Laurence Young are perfect examples of how color can be used to establish a mood. The intensity of the reds, whites, and yellows in *Pitched* suggest strong emotions, strength, the hope for movement. The more subdued colors in *Lattice Work* create a mood of peace, calm, and quiet.

Activity K: What happened when?

Diane: I'm absolutely exhausted. All I want to do is just put my feet up and forget about the whole day.

Tony: Where are the kids?

Diane: They're spending the night at your parents' house.

Tony: OK, while I finish making dinner you can tell me about your day.

Diane: I don't know where to begin. It all started after you left. As I was trying to get the kids organized for school, my boss called to say that I needed to come in early and also stay late to finish a project. Without any warning at all. To get to work early, I had to drive the kids to school instead of waiting for the school bus. Unfortunately, earlier I'd put in a load of laundry. So I had to stop that because I don't like to leave machines running when I'm not home.

Tony: Oh, man! All of this and you hadn't even left the house.

Diane: Why do you think I'm so exhausted? Anyway, before I left the house, I did manage to call mom to see if she could pick the kids up from school.

Tony: Then what?

Diane: I worked nonstop at the office. I didn't even get any lunch. I just ate an energy bar. During the morning, our clients called repeatedly about the project. That didn't help. Then, at one o'clock I got a call from the school to ask if I had sent in the permission slip for the kids to play soccer. Um … of course, I had forgotten the whole thing. So I called mom again, she went to the house, picked up the slip, and delivered it to school. As she was doing that, Nancy took the cat to the vet appointment … Of course, I had also forgotten about that. By the way … how long have you been home?

Tony: A couple of hours. The laundry is done. I got your note and started the machine right after I got home. Nancy sent me a text this afternoon to say that the cat is fine. Dinner is in the oven.

Diane: You're a sweetheart. And, luckily, tomorrow is Saturday and I don't have to go to work.

Activity L: A fender bender.

Ben: Hey, Tracy. I'm glad you finally got here. The others are waiting for us at the museum cafeteria. So tell me what happened! I'm glad you called. We were all getting worried.

Tracy: I'm so sorry. What a stupid thing to have happened!

Ben: All you said was that you were in a car accident and that you weren't hurt.

Tracy: Yeah, that's one good thing.

Ben: So … ?

Tracy: Well … anyway … to begin with … I was driving along Route 28. There was a lot of traffic and we were going pretty slowly. But it was stop-and-go … you know how that is. At one point a truck stopped very suddenly in front of me. At the same time that I stomped on my brakes, the person behind me rear-ended me. I was so shocked that, at first, I just sat there. Then someone came running to my car, opened the door, and asked me if I was OK.

Ben: Were you wearing your seatbelt?

Tracy: Of course I was. I would probably have been hurt if I hadn't. Anyway … so I got out of the car and looked at the damage. It turned out that it wasn't too bad because the car that hit me was pretty small. The bumper is dented along with the lid of the trunk. One taillight is broken.

Ben: That's not great, but what took so long?

Tracy: As soon as it happened, one of the witnesses called the police. While we waited for them to arrive, the driver of the other car and I traded insurance information. It wasn't until the police got there that we could move the cars to the side of the road. Next we had to answer a lot of questions about the crash.

Ben: How did you get here?

Tracy: I drove my car … after we finally finished with all the paperwork. The car is dinged and dented, but it's still running.

Ben: I'm so sorry about all this. But at least you're not hurt. Let's go eat lunch and then look at the exhibits. You'll forget about the accident for a while.

Activity S: Special exhibit: Two other works by Laurence Young.

Guide: These two works represent two different seasons of the year. In *Sway*, the season is autumn. Here's how Young explains the title … and I quote … "The title for *Sway* was inspired by a day when I was out walking in the woods. It was a beautiful sunlit fall day with just a slight breeze. The trees and branches seemed to *sway* in the gentle breeze," end quote. Now you understand why Young chose that title. Notice how the use of yellow, orange, reds, and a touch of purple help to create the fall scene. And the blues of the sky suggest the coolness of the air. Several things give the painting a sense of depth. First, here's the winding path that disappears into the trees. Then you see the trees that are bigger in the foreground and get smaller and smaller as you walk into the woods. And finally, the use of black and white make the foreground very detailed compared to the less defined background in the distance.

Now let's move on to the second painting. *In Season* is a summer scene. Young lives in a small ocean resort that attracts many tourists during the summer. The title

In Season refers to the months when the small town is very crowded. What we see here is a tourist or maybe one of the town's inhabitants, walking on the street and carrying a bag with something she probably bought. The woman is dressed in light summer clothing, with a hat to protect her from the sun. We see her reflection in a store window, but the reflection is much smaller than the woman herself. That and the striking black and white colors keep our eye focused on the larger image in the foreground. This painting is a beautiful example of Young's use of complementary colors: blue-orange, yellow-purple, and hot pink and lime green. And, even though we don't see other people, the reflection in the window still gives us the feeling that this is a busy time of the year.

CHAPTER 2

Activity B: Instructions or advice?

1

Ron: What do I do next?

Jack: Would you please tape up the boxes over there? Don't forget to label them.

2

Alberto: What do you want me to do?

Michelle: I need you to clean out the fridge.

3

Beth: What do you think I should do with the dog on the day the movers come?

Carmen: If I were you, I would put him into a kennel for the day. He'll be a lot calmer there.

4

Daisuke: OK, I'm ready to work. What can I do to help?

Marissa: Thanks so much for coming over. First, you can take these boxes out to the truck. Next, you can help me pack up these books.

5

Alex: I really don't know what to do with the plants. The movers won't take them.

Ben: Well, you could either move them in your car or, better yet, why not ask your neighbors if they want them?

6

Brigid: You look exhausted.

Meghan: I am. I don't know how I'm going to get all this done. Could you please help put the chairs on the truck?

7

Richard: My mom thinks I should have a garage sale to get rid of some of this stuff. What do you think?

Brian: I agree with her. That's what I'd do.

8

David: I can't possibly pack these dishes so that they won't break.

Nila: What I would do is have the movers pack them. You'll pay a little more, but it's worth it.

Activity C: What a mess!

Ernesto: This is crazy! You guys haven't done anything. We have to be out of this place in five days. We'll never get all this done!

Mike: I know, I know. Um … how about we put you in charge?

Ernesto: That's fine with me, but you can't mess around … you'll have to do what I tell you.

Park: OK, I agree.

Simon: Me too.

Ernesto: OK … I've made a checklist. But you all need to take notes so that you don't forget what you're supposed to do.

Mike, Park, Simon: OK, fine, all right …

Ernesto: First, Simon, I'm putting you in charge of the kitchen. Pack up all the dishes, pots and pans, make sure that they're packed properly, and label each box …

Simon: I'm supposed to do all this by myself? It seems to me that's the biggest job.

Park: I suppose I can help with that.

Ernesto: I guess so, Park. But you'll have plenty to do. Besides packing up your room … and we're each responsible for our own rooms … it's going to be your job to organize all the CDs and DVDs and pack them. Again, every box has to be labeled. That'll make it easier when we unpack in the new place.

Park: What about Mike? Is he going to do anything?

Ernesto: Well, I think he should be the one to help Simon with the kitchen, not you. Because he's going to be the person who's packing the car, driving the stuff to the new place, and unloading the car. Then he comes back and picks up the next load. So until the first car load is ready, he can help Simon pack up the dishes.

Simon: Hey, Ernesto. What exactly are YOU going to do?

Ernesto: Besides packing up my own stuff, I'll change the address with the post office, I'll cancel the utilities, I'll get the boxes and the tape, and I'll supervise.

Mike: And who's taking all the posters off the walls? Couldn't you do that too?

Ernesto: Sure. Why not? Now, here's what I think about the cleaning. If we move all the stuff in the next three days, then we'll have two more days to clean the whole place. Park and Simon, I think you should clean the kitchen. You always made such a mess that it's only fair if you clean it up. Mike, you can patch the nail holes in the walls and fix the doorbell. Park, let's see … you wash the windows. And I'll mop the floors.

Park: Why are we doing all this? Aren't you being just a little too picky?

Ernesto: You want the security deposit back or not? This place has to be in perfect shape when we leave. Otherwise you can forget about getting the money back.

Activity K: Where?

1

Jin: Where are we going to meet them?

Brianna: I told them we'd meet at the coffee shop across the street from the bookstore.

2

Beth: Where should I put this?

Francine: You can hang it on the wall in the living room. Next to the picture window.

3

Kent: Where's my new jacket?

Sean: Let's see. What did I do with that? Oh yeah, it's in the closet.

4

Tim: Where did you put my cell phone?

Anna: I'm not sure. I think it's on the kitchen counter.

5

Steve: Where, exactly, am I supposed to pick up the packages?

Michael: I already told you. In the office building at the corner of Elm and Standish, on the fifth floor.

6

Angela: Where is Jimmy?

River: I told him he could play in the pool with the other kids.

7

Mateo: Where should we put this chest of drawers?

Emily: Hm … Good question. How about we put it right over there, under the window?

8

Malcolm: Where do we pick up the bus for New York?

Young-Hwan: I checked online and the best place is at South Station.

9

Rita: Where did you see tacos? I'm really in the mood for tacos tonight.

Judy: On the menu. Let's see. It's right here, under the specials of the day.

10

Cesar: Where did you go on vacation?

Wanda: I spent three weeks in China. It was a fabulous trip.

Activity L: Moving into a new place.

Sarah: I can't believe we're finally here. It's a good thing the girls and Percy are at your parents'. Can you imagine if they were running around here? OK … so where do we start?

Jamal: I have no idea. I'm not good at this sort of thing.

Sarah: *[laughs]* You always say that when you don't want to do something. OK. I'll organize. Let's see … how about we set up the kitchen first.

Jamal: I'm not so sure. I think it would be better if we unpacked the clothes and the toys. Once they're in the closets, we'll get rid of all these big boxes in the living room.

Sarah: Good point. I guess we could do the kids' room first and then move to ours. OK. Why don't you put the toys into the toy box. Then you can put Janie's stuffed animals on the shelf above her bed and Alyssa's dolls on the shelf by the window. And all of their books can go on these bookshelves. I'll arrange their clothes in the closets and in the drawers. This shouldn't take long. Then we'll go on to our room. *[some time later]*

Sarah: Wow! I'm exhausted. What about you?

Jamal: Yeah, let's take a break … Do you really think we'll like living in this part of town?

Sarah: It's a little late to ask that question … but yeah, I think this is perfect for all of us. It's a relatively safe neighborhood, the park is up the street, the girls' school is just a couple of blocks away, and we're within walking distance of the grocery store.

Jamal: You're right. I just get a little nervous about all this every once in a while. This was a really big move. I hope we did the right thing.

Sarah: Look, I know that we're going to miss our friends and our old neighborhood. But it's not like they're all

that far away. And we're living a little closer to your parents. That's really convenient when we need help with the kids and the cats … like this weekend.

Jamal: The cats? I don't know …

Sarah: Yeah … the cats … plural. We promised the kids we'd get Percy a companion. So that's what we're going to do.

Jamal: Well … uh … why not. It's probably better for Percy if he has someone to play with when we're not home.

Sarah: Agreed. To get back to the point, this is a really good house in a terrific neighborhood.

Jamal: And the real bonus is that we're on the bus line for work. And I must admit that I like all the trees and the closed-in backyard. I guess change is good.

Sarah: You don't have to convince ME. I already love it here.

Activity U: We agree … this is the house for us.

Lori: I know you disagree with me, but I really don't think we should buy this house.

Carl: Look, it's the right price, it's the perfect size, um … it has a great yard, it's on a quiet street, and best of all, it's close to work.

Lori: All of that's true, but you have to admit that the place is a mess. Every room has to be repainted …

Carl: You're right, but that's not a big deal. We can do it ourselves.

Lori: Agreed. But what about all the plumbing problems?

Carl: I'll give you that one. We'll have to hire a plumber.

Lori: Now you're making sense. But that'll be very expensive. And the windows are in miserable shape, and the whole master bathroom has to be redone.

Carl: I'll grant you that. Yes, it'll take some money. But we can bring in someone to replace the windows and I'll redo the bathroom.

Lori: Are you serious? When are you planning to do all that? Before you go to work at six or after you get home at eight for a late dinner?

Carl: Hm … I hadn't thought of that. The house is very interesting, but I can see your point. It has too many problems. Let's keep looking.

[Different Day]

Carl: So what do you think?

Lori: Well … this house is in perfect condition. The kitchen has been totally remodeled, the roof is new, it has a garage with a door that leads into the kitchen … it has three bedrooms …

Carl: But?

Lori: Well … ah … it's just that … well … I was looking for something with a little more character. This house looks like every other house in the neighborhood. It's kinda boring.

Carl: Yes, but it's beautiful and it has everything we want …

Lori: Except for a fireplace. I really wanted a fireplace.

Carl: Oh come on. That's ridiculous. This is the first time you said anything about a fireplace! We don't need a fireplace. What we need is a house we can afford, one that doesn't need any work, the right number of rooms …

Lori: OK, OK. Ah … the fireplace just occurred to me. But I see your point. I have to say that this is the best property we've seen. The kitchen is great for entertaining. And the deck is fabulous … and it's very private because of all the trees.

Carl: I can picture our stuff in here. And since we don't have to spend any money on repairs, maybe we could buy new furniture for the living room.

Lori: That's a great idea, honey. And maybe a new dining room table. OK, I'm convinced. We agree. This is the house for us!

CHAPTER 3

Activity B: I can't wait to eat!

James: The table looks great, honey. And the food smells soooo good. I can't wait to eat!

Sandra: Stop nibbling. You won't be hungry when it's time to eat. You know … I couldn't have done all this if you hadn't done the shopping yesterday. That made all the difference.

James: Do you think we overdid it? This seems like a huge amount of food for just the six of us.

Sandra: That's not a problem. Everyone can take home some leftovers. … I can't wait to meet Yoshiro's parents. I hope they like all this American food. I was thinking of including something Japanese … but I couldn't figure out what to do.

James: Of course they'll like the food. You're a terrific cook and … besides … they've lived in this country for many years. After all, Yoshiro was born here, so I'm sure this isn't the first time they've been invited to a Thanksgiving dinner.

Sandra: I just hope they like us. Yoshiro is so important to Karen. I have a feeling they're going to make an announcement today.

James: An announcement? What're you talking about?

Sandra: Well, you know … I think they might announce their engagement. Karen said she had something important to tell us. So … since they're really serious about each other, it wouldn't surprise me if they wanted to get married.

James: Married! But Karen is only twenty-five! She's too young to get married!

Sandra: I guess you're forgetting that I was only twenty-one when I married you. Karen can't be your little girl forever. She's a young woman with the beginnings of a good career in law. And Yoshiro's already well established as a software engineer.

James: I suppose … But he works for a computer gaming company … what kind of career is that?

Sandra: You're kidding, right? Don't be so old-fashioned. There's lots of money to be made in designing computer games and he likes what he does. I think that Karen and Yoshiro make a terrific couple. They have a lot in common and they've been going out for almost two years.

James: Well … I have to admit that I really like Yoshiro. I always like watching football with him. He cares about sports and knows a lot about them. I wanna keep going to baseball games with him.

Sandra: See … you're already planning to spend more time with him. I don't know about you, but I'd love to have some more grandchildren. I love Tony's kids, but they live so far away …

James: I wouldn't start counting on grandchildren. Karen's pretty ambitious and I think she'll want to continue in her career before she gets tied down with kids.

Sandra: We'll see. There's the doorbell. Let's go welcome our possible new in-laws!

Activity C: It's nice to finally meet you!

Segment 1

Sandra: Welcome to our home. Please come in.

Karen: Mom, Dad, I'd like you to meet Yoshiro's parents, Hana and Shiro Matsuo. Mr. and Mrs. Matsuo, these are my parents Sandra and James O'Donnell.

James: It's so nice to finally meet you. We've heard a lot about you. We're glad you could join us for dinner. Karen and Yoshiro, we haven't seen you in almost a month. We'll have to catch up.

Shiro: It's nice for us to meet you also. Thank you for inviting us.

Yoshiro: Yes, I'm sorry I wasn't able to go to the game last weekend. But my job …

James: Don't worry about it. I'm sure we'll have plenty more chances to go to football games.

Segment 2

Hana: Mrs. O'Donnell, this is a small gift … a rosemary plant … Karen tells us that you like to cook, so …

Sandra: Oh, you shouldn't have. Thank you so much. It's very lovely and the ceramic pot is beautiful. I'll put it on the window sill in the kitchen. Now I'll have rosemary for the entire winter. And please call me Sandra.

James: First, let's make ourselves comfortable. Let me take your coats and then we can go into the living room for some appetizers. Mr. Matsuo, your coat?

Shiro: Please call me Shiro. After all, our children are dating, so we can also be a bit less formal.

James: That's sounds good to me, Shiro. Feel free to call me James. What can I offer you to drink?

Segment 3

Sandra: So … Shiro and Hana … Yoshiro tells us that you like to go hiking.

Hana: Yes, we like to spend time in nature. So we go hiking very often.

James: Where do you go?

Shiro: It depends. Sometimes we drive into the mountains or to a national park …

Hana: … but we also drive to the ocean and hike in the dunes.

Sandra: James and I like to go camping. Maybe we could get together sometime and combine camping with hiking. That would be fun.

Shiro: Do you like to fish, James?

James: Do I like to fish? I love it. But I don't get to do it often enough.

Shiro: I am a fisherman. If we go camping, you and I could be in charge of catching dinner.

Sandra: That sounds like a great idea. But, knowing James, I think I'll still pack some food, just in case …

Hana: That's a good idea. Shiro likes to fish, but the fish don't always cooperate.

Yoshiro: Hey, what about us? We like camping and hiking too.

James: Well … you can come along if you want.

Activity L: What does that mean?

1

OK, kids. I've had enough. Knock it off! All this noise is making me crazy.

2

I'm not surprised you're exhausted and irritable. You work twenty-four/seven. I think your boss is being unreasonable.

3

I'm turning over a new leaf. I'm going to eat more fruit and vegetables and I'm going to the gym at least three times a week. I've gotta get into better shape.

4

I can tell you what roads to take. I've done it many times. I know this region like the back of my hand.

5

You need help transferring your pictures? Here … I'll show you. It's a piece of cake. It'll just take a few minutes for you to learn how to do it.

6

I bent over backwards for her. But she didn't appreciate anything I did. No matter what I did to help, nothing was good enough for her.

7

Congratulations everyone! After a couple of years of struggling, we're in the black again. And our sales projections for this coming year are even higher.

8

I know it's difficult. But you have to keep your chin up. If you work hard, things'll get better.

Activity M: Everything is delicious!

Shiro: Everything is delicious, Sandra.

James: Yes, compliments to the chef. I wish I could just keep eating.

Sandra: Thank you. I'm glad you like everything.

Karen: Leave some room for dessert. Mom makes wonderful pies.

Hana: I particularly like the Brussels sprouts. How did you prepare them?

Sandra: There's nothing to it. Just take off the outer leaves, put some olive oil, salt, and pepper on them and roast them in the oven. I think they're better roasted than boiled.

Hana: I agree. I'm going to try that next time I make them.

James: Could you pass the bread, please? Thanks. So … Karen. How's your new job?

Karen: Well … to tell the truth … I have some mixed feelings about it. I'm not crazy about my boss. He's not easy to talk to and he doesn't seem to have a sense of humor. But it's OK. I'm just getting my feet wet. But let's not talk business.

Shiro: Have you found an apartment yet?

Karen: Well … not yet. I'm still staying with my friend Angela. Everything I've looked at costs an arm and a leg. So I'll just keep looking for something more affordable. Besides … Could you pass the pepper, Mom? Thanks. This turkey is fabulous. Can I take some home with me?

Sandra: Of course. I'm counting on everyone taking leftovers home.

James: About your apartment. We'll talk later. Maybe we can help out. In any case, I'm so glad that we could all spend Thanksgiving together. Karen and Yoshiro have been seeing each other for a while … so …

Karen: Actually, Dad, everyone … Yoshiro and I wanna make an announcement … um …

Yoshiro: What Karen is trying to say is that … that … I've asked her to marry me and … and … she said "yes."

Sandra: Congratulations! I'm so happy for you … for all of us!

James: So you finally popped the question, Yoshiro. I was beginning to wonder how long it would take.

Sandra: Come on, James. Tell the truth. You didn't have an inkling about this until I mentioned the possibility to you.

Shiro: Let's make a toast to Karen and Yoshiro. Here's to a bright future.

Sandra: And now it's time for dessert. Help yourselves.

Hana: Yoshiro, Karen, I'm so happy. You two make a lovely couple.

James: Have you set the wedding date yet?

Yoshiro: Well … we're thinking about June. That gives us plenty of time to make the preparations and … um … to find an apartment that's big enough for the two of us.

Activity U: Eating healthy.

Nutritionist: OK, so today we'll talk about what we call MyPlate. Our topic is good eating habits. Look at the image of the U.S. Department of Agriculture model for healthy eating. What do you notice about it?

Luis: There are four different food groups on the plate and a separate section for dairy. I guess that means that we should eat different kinds of foods.

Nutritionist: That's correct. What else?

Melanie: Well … the four sections on the plate are a different size. Are they trying to say that we should eat more of some foods and less of other foods?

Nutritionist: You're both right. You just identified the two main messages communicated by this model: Eat different kinds of foods and don't eat the same amounts from each food category. So, for example, on the left side of the plate, we should eat more vegetables than fruit. On the right side, we should eat more grains than

protein. And we should not eat or drink a lot of dairy. But the other message we get from the divided plate is that we shouldn't have huge portions (not more than you can fit on a normal plate) because huge portions make you gain weight.

Luis: Um … I don't think I know what's meant by grains or what foods are considered … ah … protein.

Nutritionist: Well … foods made from grains are things like bread, rice, cereal, pasta, tortillas, chips. When you eat grains, it's better to eat whole-wheat bread, oatmeal, or brown rice. Proteins are foods like meat, fish, beans, nuts, eggs, and tofu. And, of course, dairy includes milk, yogurt, and cheese.

Melanie: I don't get the fruit thing. I thought fruit was really good for you, so why should we eat less of it than vegetables? I don't like vegetables much, but I really like fruit.

Nutritionist: You're right, fruit is good for you, in moderation. But remember that there's a lot of sugar in fruit, so you don't want to overdo it. Try to limit the amount of sugar you get from foods.

Luis: All this is kinda depressing. Does that mean I can't pig out or eat my favorite foods like pizza, tacos, burritos whenever I feel like it?

Nutritionist: That's not what it means. It just means that you shouldn't eat foods like that every day, that you shouldn't "pig out," as you say, that you shouldn't eat out a lot, especially in fast-food places, that it's better to eat regular meals than grabbing a bit to eat whenever you feel like it, and, if you have a sweet tooth, you should be careful about eating lots of desserts.

Melanie: So this doesn't mean that I have to eat like a bird, right?

Nutritionist: Of course not. It just means that you should practice moderation. That's the key: moderation. Eat smaller portions of a variety of foods. So, for example, if you're in the food court at the mall, don't overeat. Don't let your eyes be bigger than your stomach. Maybe just order one piece of pizza … if you haven't had pizza in a long time … and a small salad. And for heaven's sake, don't drink a lot of soda. There's way too much sugar in stuff like that. Water is good for you. OK … next time we'll talk about food preparation and I'll show you how to make even vegetables taste really good, Melanie.

CHAPTER 4

Activity B: A family reunion.

Description A

I think everyone had a blast. There were like a hundred of us and we hadn't seen each other in two years. We basically spent three days eating and drinking, practically from morning until night. All the grandkids and cousins played and ran around until they were exhausted. The only ones that maybe didn't have such a good time were the teenagers. They looked bored a lot of the time. And, oh yeah, they seemed more interested in looking at their cell phones. They stood at different places in the park and texted each other. It was a bit bizarre.

Description B

I think the reunion was a huge success. And the food was amazing, if I do say so myself. Of course that's because I was put in charge of the grilling. And there was something for everyone: hamburgers, hot dogs, steaks, even some lamb chops. And lots of sides, of course. Mary brought her famous potato salad, Charlie made a pot of his vegetarian chili, and there were different kinds of salads; we had corn on the cob and vegetables. And the desserts were absolutely delicious. We bought pastries from a local bakery. And for the kids, we also had different flavors of ice cream.

Description C

I can't believe what it took to make this reunion happen. I'm not sure I could do it again. But it was my family's turn to be in charge and I couldn't very well back down. So, like it or not, it took us almost two months to organize everything. There were hotel reservations to be made, a bakery to contact for the desserts, an extra freezer to rent for the ice cream, people to call, games to organize, family to pick up from the airport, the train and bus stations, well, you get the idea. And, the day before everyone arrived, I was still making last-minute arrangements on the phone, confirming reservations on the Internet, and cooking, all at the same time! It was incredibly hectic. I guess it was worth it. Everyone seems to have had a good time.

Description D

I think reunions are boring. OK, so I got to see some of my cousins and we ate lots of good food. To have more fun, we got in different parts of the park and started texting each other. It was very funny. We could say anything we wanted to and no one knew what we were talking about. But the most exciting thing that happened was the fight between my aunt Hilda and my mother. They drive each other crazy and they always find something to freak out about. I'm not totally sure what the argument was, but I think it had something to do with the fact that aunt Hilda did absolutely nothing to help with the reunion. So they screeched at each other until my father stepped in. The rest of the family didn't think it was funny, but my cousins and I loved it. Hilda and my mother are always at each other's

throats, so this was nothing new. But at least it gave us something to text about. Other than gossiping about everybody we don't like.

Activity C: The details of the reunion.

1

OK. So the calendar for the reunion is finally set. Here's what's happening for the three days. Everyone arrives on Friday. John and the kids are getting here by bus at 2:15. Aunt Beth is going to pick them up. Karen and Charlie are taking the ferry. Alex has to go pick them up at the pier at 11:00. I'm going to the airport to get Max and Aunt Phyllis. Their plane lands at 1:30. Your cousins are driving and should be here around noon. Just in time for lunch. Joanne's train is getting here at 10:30. I think that Alex can pick her up before he goes to the pier. Everybody else is getting here by car in time for dinner at 7:00. Saturday is not as complicated. Basically we all meet at the house for breakfast at 9:00. Then people can socialize until lunch. The caterer is arriving at 11:30 to set everything up. We should eat around 12:30. At 2:30, the buses are picking us up for a tour of the city. We'll get back to the house by 5:00. People can do whatever they want until the barbecue at 6:30.

Sunday is the last day and it's jam packed with stuff. Everyone is on their own for breakfast. We'll meet at 10:30 at the lake. Those who want to swim can do so; the rest of us will get lunch ready. The food will already be at the cabin, so it's just a matter of making sandwiches and taking the salads out of the refrigerator. We'll eat at 1:00. The afternoon is open for napping, swimming, playing volleyball, or taking walks. But everyone has to meet back at the cabin by 5:00 for the return trip to the city. Our final dinner will be at the restaurant. Our reservations are for 7:30.
We can't plan Monday until we know when everyone is leaving. So let's not worry about that right now.

2

What a nightmare. I've finally sorted out what everyone is doing. Thank goodness that we have five volunteers besides you and me to put this reunion together. I think I'd go crazy if we had to do it by ourselves. So here's what our volunteers are doing. You said that Beth is gonna pick up John and the kids at the bus station. And Alex is going to the pier to pick up Karen and Charlie, and then he's going to pick up Joanne at the train station.

Grandpa Sid volunteered to schedule the tour bus for our excursion around the city. Aunt Beth is helping me to decide on the menu and then she'll order the food from the caterer. Grandma Cynthia will be supervising the kids as much as possible. Sid said he would babysit little Zoe because he's crazy about her. Uncle Rick said he'd do the grilling on Saturday night and he'd help Beth make the salads for the picnic at the lake. Cynthia wants to be in charge of serving drinks and making the coffee at all the meals. She and Sid agreed to do some of the shopping. He'll pick up the grilling meats, she'll buy the food for the picnic, and he'll also get the bags of ice for the coolers. Alex wants to buy the drinks because he doesn't trust anyone else to make a good selection. Rick'll call the restaurant for the Sunday dinner reservation and he'll drive the grandparents to the lake. And, most importantly, Alex is gonna rent the tent in case it rains on Saturday. That about does it. Let's hope they all come through.

Activity K: Did you hear?

Conversation A

Anna: Can you believe it? Did you hear Petra say that she quit her job and plans to become a painter?

Emily: Well, I didn't actually hear it myself. But Giulia told me. It's unbelievable. She's giving up a great salary to live on the beach and paint.

Anna: I'm stunned by the whole thing. So you think I should ask to be considered for her job?

Emily: Why don't you wait and see if she actually goes through with it.

Conversation B

Allen: You'll never guess what just happened. I was jogging along the lake path and saw Liam sitting on a bench with a very attractive woman. That really infuriates me. His wife is such a nice person.

Matt: Well … it wouldn't be the first time that he looks at other women. I don't know how his wife puts up with it.

Sue: I don't believe you two. Maybe the woman you saw him with is a colleague or a relative. And you have no evidence that he's ever been unfaithful to his wife.

Allen: But he always seems to be looking!

Sue: And what about you! I saw your eyes follow that woman who just walked by. You should both be ashamed of yourselves!

Conversation C

David: Did you hear that Benjamin is losing his house? It seems that he has lots of financial problems and can't keep up with his expenses.

Brian: I'm so sorry to hear that. Benjamin is a very nice guy and he works so hard. What happened?

David: Well … I heard that he's a really big shopper. Any time he sees something he likes, he gets on the Internet and buys it. And he always uses credit cards.

Brian: That'll do it. Expenses like that are hard to get away from. Is there anything we can do to help him?

David: Hmm … we could go to his yard sale. I heard that he's selling most of his belongings for very good prices. We might find something interesting and help him out at the same time.

Brian: Sounds like a plan.

Conversation D

Rita: I couldn't wait to tell you the great news. My granddaughter Aicha just got admitted to veterinary school. I'm thrilled.

Cathy: Wow! That's fabulous. Congratulate her for me. I know how much she loves animals.

Kevin: She'll be really good as a vet. When she was a little kid, she was always saving some animal or other. She has a good heart.

Rita: You're right. And she's also very smart. I'm so proud of her.

Conversation E

Michael: Did you hear that Oliver flunked the chem final exam?

Young-Jin: No! That's terrible. He'll have to retake the course.

Michael: Actually, I'm not too surprised. Oliver usually studies very hard. But this time, he was so preoccupied with his new girlfriend that his studies really suffered. He should have worked harder.

Young-Jin: How do you know all that? How do you even know that he failed the exam?

Michael: I heard it from Simon who heard it from Isabella who heard it from a reliable source. And I've seen how infatuated he is with Erika.

Young-Jin: That doesn't mean anything. I think this is just a rumor and I wouldn't repeat it if I were you.

Conversation F

Diane: I can't believe that Dorrie wants to start a rock band. That's just crazy!

Brenda: What do you mean, a rock band. She doesn't even know how to sing.

Diane: But she thinks she does. Her music teacher told her that she had a pretty good voice and now she imagines that she's wonderful.

Brenda: And who are the other members of this new band?

Diane: She doesn't know yet. But she's thinking about Jessie on lead guitar, No'am on bass guitar, and her brother on percussion.

Brenda: Her brother? He's really lousy on the drums.

Diane: That's OK. Dorrie doesn't really know how to sing!

Activity N: What are they arguing about?

Conversation 1

Daughter: Mom, can I get a cell phone?

Mother: No, I think you're too young. And besides, we can't afford it right now.

Daughter: You never let me buy anything I want. All my friends have cells.

Mother: I never let you buy anything you want? We just bought you a new bike.

Daughter: That's different. You only buy the things you agree with. You don't care about what *I* really want. I didn't even want the stupid bike!

Mother: That's not what you said last month.

Conversation 2

Aaron: Why did you call this meeting?

Jamal: Because I'm sick to death of doing everything around here. I cook, clean the apartment, straighten up the living room, wash the dishes. And you guys just sit around and do nothing.

Randall: Nobody asked you to do all that. So what do you wanna do about it?

Jamal: I live here too and I refuse to live in your mess. So, either you start helping around here or I'll stop cooking for you and cleaning up after you.

Aaron: But you're the only one who knows how to cook.

Jamal: OK. Then if I cook, you do the dishes and clean the kitchen. And if I straighten up the living room, then you two can dust and vacuum.

Conversation 3

Wife: We're spending too much money.

Husband: You mean *I* spend too much money.

Wife: Why do you always take it personally when I talk about money?

Husband: Because you don't want me to spend every weekend playing golf.

Wife: I don't care if you play golf. But you're spending too much money on all the equipment. Why did you have to buy another set of clubs last week? And how many sets of sunglasses, hats, and gloves do you really need?

Conversation 4

Father: I don't want to argue about this anymore!

Daughter: I still don't see why Eric can have his own room and I have to share my room with Stephanie.

Father: I already explained that to you. We only have two bedrooms for you kids and it makes sense that the girls have one room and the boy the other.

Daughter: Well it doesn't make any sense to me. I'm the oldest and I never have any privacy!

Father: Don't raise your voice to me. If you want more privacy, then stay in your room when your sister is doing something else. Like right now. She's outside with her friends. This would be a good time to go to your room.

Conversation 5

Mother: Mario, come in and start your homework.

Mario: Just a little more time. I'm trying to practice my hook shot.

Mother: I know you think that basketball is more important than homework, but it's not.

Mario: Oh, come on, another half hour.

Mother: I'm not going to repeat myself. Get in here right now! You told me you had to write a book report. Did you finish reading the book?

Mario: Hmmm … Yea, but I left it at school.

Mother: OK. That's it. I'll take you back to school to get it. Then you do your homework. And … no basketball for the next three days!

Conversation 6

Tamara: I can't believe that you borrowed my sweater without asking.

Jules: Well, you weren't home and I didn't think you'd mind.

Tamara: You didn't think I'd mind? What are you talking about! We had a deal: we don't borrow each other's clothes.

Jules: Why are you making such a big deal out of this?

Tamara: Because I was going to wear the sweater tonight and now I can't because you got a big stain on it!

Activity O: Family spat.

Beth: Knock it off, you two. What's all this yelling about? We can hear you out in the backyard.

T.J.: He took my cell and I want it back!

Uncle Chris: You're not getting it back until you have the courtesy to spend five minutes talking to your grandparents. They haven't seen you in a long time and you could show some respect.

T.J.: Mom, he's not my parent. He can't tell me what to do!

Uncle Chris: But this is my house and, while you're in it, you'll do as I say!

Beth: Stop it! Both of you. Everyone's listening!

T.J.: I don't care. I want my cell. I was just texting a friend.

Beth: Young man, I AM your parent. Now march yourself out there and have a nice chat with gramma and grampa. Then you'll get your phone back.

Beth: Chris, give me the phone. What were you thinking … getting into a shouting match with a 15-year old?

Uncle Chris: Somebody has to teach him some manners. I'm his uncle and he's in my house. I don't have to put up with his rude behavior.

Beth: Oh! So now you're accusing me of not teaching him good manners! You're worse than he is! You're supposed to be the adult.

Uncle Chris: Let's face it. These reunions are not what they used to be. The kids are bored, they don't want to talk to anyone, they don't want to play volleyball, and all they do is text their friends who seem to be more important than the family. You're my sister and I love you. But I'm not sure I can do this again.

Beth: You've never been crazy about the reunions. But they happen only every two years and it's the only time we get to see everyone.

Uncle Chris: You know, it occurs to me that maybe we should just send all the teenagers to the movies down the street. They'd have more fun, the adults could catch up with each other, and the smaller children can play together.

Beth: It's a thought. But I'm a little nervous about letting the kids go off by themselves.

Uncle Chris: I could go with them. That way I could make sure that they don't get into trouble.

Beth: Fat chance! You just want to get out of socializing. This is your house and it would be rude for you to leave. No, I think Mark would be glad to go with them.

Uncle Chris: OK. But would you consider holding the reunion at a more interesting place next time? Like maybe at an ocean resort where there's something to do for everyone?

Beth: That's not the worst idea you've had. We'll put it to a family vote right after we eat.

CHAPTER 5

Activity B: What's that class like?

Conversation 1

Ginny: So, how are you liking your classes?

Sonja: Really well, actually. The real surprise is how much I like my Web design class. I really just took it because it worked with my schedule, but I love it. I think everyone should take this class. No matter what your major is or what kind of job you think you'll have, knowing this stuff will come in really handy in the future.

Conversation 2

Samuel: You're taking Intro to Psych, aren't you?

Tyrone: Uh huh.

Samuel: And you're doing OK, right?

Tyrone: Yeah, definitely. We have readings to do for Mondays, little group and individual presentations to give on Wednesdays, and quizzes on Fridays. And if you don't do well on a quiz, you can study some more and retake a different version of it the following Tuesday.

Conversation 3

Eileen: So, how's your astronomy class?

Kevin: It's OK, I guess.

Eileen: You guess?

Kevin: Yeah, well I guess, I wasn't really thinking when I registered for it. I was expecting a class where you talk about the stars, and about how the constellations got their names, and stuff like that. And I thought we'd just spend a lot of time looking at the sky. But it *is* a physics course, after all, and it has a lot of math in it. That's not really my thing, so I find it a little dry …

Conversation 4

Delia: I'm loving my American history class this fall. I'm thinking of taking the second level with Dr. Murphy next semester.

Armando: Good luck with that.

Delia: What do you mean?

Armando: I took it last year and it just about killed me. We had a huge textbook, and every week we also had several articles to read. Some of those were really theoretical – I couldn't even understand what the authors were saying half the time. And we had to write these papers where we applied the articles to the Civil War or one of the World Wars. I felt lost a lot of the time. Murphy talks really fast, too, but she *was* always willing to help me. I spent a lot of time in her office.

Conversation 5

Aram: I've heard you do most of your work in groups in that Cultural Anthropology course. That's cool.

Theo: Well, I guess I wouldn't say "*most* of your work." You *do* do a group research project and a group presentation in front of the class. I really liked those 'cause it helped me get to know some people I'm still friends with now. But you also do three exams and four short reports, and for those, you're on your own …

Conversation 6

Paula: Hey, I just found this course called Art and Culture in the 20th Century. I'm really excited to take it.

All my classes have been OK so far, but I'd really like to take a class where I get to draw and paint and make stuff. My classes haven't required much creativity so far, and I miss that.

Deb: Well, I'm not sure that class is exactly what you think it is. You don't actually get to *make* anything. It's more listening to music, and looking at paintings, and stuff like that. You do get to talk about how the art makes you feel, and you give your own interpretations of what a work of art might mean. That's kinda creative.

Paula: Thanks for telling me. I didn't quite understand what it was. I think I'm still gonna take it, though. I think it'll still have some of what I wanted.

Activity C: What should I take?

Advisor: So, Maria, you're going to register for three courses for next term, right?

Maria: Yeah, I think I can handle that now. That How to Succeed in College course you recommended is really helping me. Before taking it, I never knew how to take good notes, and I was pretty bad at taking tests, too. For instance, now I see that I wasn't reading test questions carefully enough, and I didn't get what the prof was asking for. No wonder my test grades weren't so great when I started here.

Advisor: I'm glad you found it valuable. And a course like that also helps you understand what U.S. academic culture is all about. So, what about next term?

Maria: Well, first, do you think it's a good idea to take Business Statistics now? I don't really like math all that much, but the stats course is required for business majors, so maybe I should just get it over with. What do you think?

Advisor: Have you taken our math placement test, Maria?

Maria: Yeah, I did that last spring. I placed into Math 120, but I thought I'd put it off a while. I guess I'm really nervous about math …

Advisor: Well, Business Stats has Math 120 as a prerequisite, so you have to take that before you can take the stats course. Listen, I suggest you take 120 next term, and then take the stats course right after that, while the math is still fresh in your mind. If you keep up in the Math course, I think you might even like it, and then you'll feel prepared for stats. You're a good student. I know you can do it.

Maria: Thanks – that makes me feel better. I'll take your advice. And I know I can always get help from the Math Center if I need it. So, besides that, I was considering that Contemporary Issues in Economics course. Do you think that's a good idea?

Advisor: Absolutely. It presents things from a U.S. point of view, but when you're back working in Ecuador, your colleagues will be glad you can explain how Americans look at certain issues. That should be a "plus" for you. In my opinion, that's an excellent choice. And for your third course?

Maria: Well, I'm really interested in literature, so I think I'm gonna take that course on Shakespeare. Everybody says the prof is really good.

Advisor: Hmm, Shakespeare …

Maria: You don't think that's a good idea?

Advisor: Well, Shakespeare is a great writer, and his language is beautiful, but it can be a challenge to understand, even for native speakers of English. I'd like to see you take another lit course before you jump into Shakespeare. Have you considered this course on the American Short Story? If I were you, I'd take something like that first. I don't want you to get in over your head.

Maria: Oh, I didn't even notice that one. The course description sounds really interesting. Thanks for pointing it out! …

Activity K: Can you take a hint?

1

A: What an *interesting* outfit to wear to a job interview!

B: I'm glad you like it. I really want to show them how creative I am.

2

A: *Most* of the sources you use in your paper are really good …

B: Are there some that you think I should eliminate, maybe?

3

A: This is a good paper. You'll probably proofread it one more time before you turn it in, right?

B: No, I think I'm good. Should I put it on your desk?

4

A: You know, *most* people write to the professor first to *ask* whether he or she is willing to write the recommendation.

B: Oh, I'm sure she will. I'm just gonna leave the form in her mailbox.

5

A: Have you got a *really* good grasp of the vocabulary on page 243?

B: I'm not sure … But I'll make sure I do before taking the test!

6

A: In my experience, lots of students have *problems* when they take those two courses at the same time.

B: Hmm. Maybe I should put off the statistics course till next fall.

7

A: Wow, gas prices are just getting higher and higher, aren't they?

B: Hey, let me pay this time. I really appreciate all of the rides you've been giving me.

8

A: Well, I'm glad you stopped by. I'm sure you've got lots of things to do today, so I'll let you go …

B: No, really, I've got plenty of time. Can you tell me about the book you're writing?

Activity L: Helpful advice.

Marco: Hi, Rita, nice to see you! Would you like to sit down?

Rita: Sure! I saw you over here, and just thought I'd stop and say hi. Hey, I saw Don Baker today, and he says you're doing an internship with him!

Marco: Yes, it was so nice of him to offer me one. He's a friend of my dad's, did you know that?

Rita: Yes, I did. So, what exactly are you doing?

Marco: Well, some of it isn't that interesting – proofreading documents and delivering them to lawyers' offices. But I also get to do some legal research, and that's really cool.

Rita: What are your work hours?

Marco: I work every day from 8:00 'til 4:00.

Rita: Are you having any trouble getting there by 8:00?

Marco: Well, I'm not really a morning person, so sometimes I'm not quite on time. I'm never more than 20 minutes late though. And I don't think Don really minds. He's known me since I was a kid.

Rita: This is a little different, though. Now you're interacting in a professional setting, and he's your boss. I don't think I'd just assume that he's OK with it.

Marco: Come to think of it, I have seen him look at his watch a couple of times when I stopped in to say good morning. I might've messed up here. What do you think?

Rita: I think it's quite possible. He may not want to say anything because you're his friend's son, but I'm guessing your lateness might bother him.

Marco: Oh no, this is really bad. What should I do now?

Rita: If I were you, I'd tell him that this is your first internship, and you've been having trouble getting organized. You know, you've been late several times, and you're really sorry – and that it won't happen again.

Marco: Thanks, Rita. I'll do that first thing tomorrow morning.

Rita: And then I'd advise you to make sure it *doesn't* happen again.

Marco: From now on, I'll be on time every day. I really do want to make a good impression.

Rita: I think that's a good decision. You know, if you don't show that you're taking this job seriously, it will be hard for Don to recommend you for another one. And that would be a real shame.

Marco: Boy, am I glad you happened to stop in here today! Thanks a lot, Rita.

Activity T: Adult education.

Kevin: You're listening to WTLK talk radio. Today's topic is "Getting educated in America." Next I'll be talking to Carla, from River City. Hello, Carla, you're on the air.

Carla: Hi, Kevin. I'm calling to say how … *frustrated* I am about getting a college education in this country. It seems like everything is, um, set up for people between 18 and 25 years old. Well, uh, I'm pretty convinced that if you don't get your degree then, you'll find it almost impossible to get it later.

Kevin: Carla, you make a good point. Most of our educational opportunities seem to be geared toward young people who have few other responsibilities and who are going to school full time. So, what's your story?

Carla: OK, so I had a kid pretty much right out of high school, and my husband and I have been working full time ever since. And then we had another kid last year. Um, don't get me wrong, we don't regret it, and we're doing OK money-wise, but there's no way either of us can quit work. And if I don't have a college degree, I'll never get promoted.

Kevin: Carla, have you considered going to college part time?

Carla: See, this is what I'm talking about. I can't take more than one class at a time, because of the kids. And if I took one class each semester, it would take me … like … I don't know … about 10 years to get a BA! I just don't see how I'm ever gonna manage it.

Kevin: I see what you mean. I'm sorry if that felt like a dumb suggestion. OK, what about this? If I were you, I'd look into some other ways to get a college degree.

It would be a good idea to find some of the colleges that offer courses online. And we're talking about real courses from real colleges here. That might also be less expensive.

Carla: You know what? I might even prefer to take classes that way. And it would sure help with our child-care problems …

Kevin: And here's something else you might not know. Some colleges actually offer course credits for work or life experience. I'll bet you could get in on that, too.

Carla: Wow. I had no idea.

Kevin: I'm sure you can find out about this stuff by going online and maybe by talking to an advisor from a local college. There are just so many benefits to having a degree … I'd like to see you find a way.

Carla: Look, I know you've got other calls to take, but I wanna thank you for your suggestions. I'm gonna go online right now, and see what I can find. I know it won't be easy, but I actually feel sort of optimistic …

CHAPTER 6

Activity B: Geography in the news.

1

When children write letters to Santa Claus and address them to the North Pole, they should specify that they mean the *geographic* North Pole, which is a fixed point, and not the *magnetic* North Pole, which moves constantly because of changes in the earth's core.

2

Strict regulations continue in some 20 eastern and midwestern states to stop the spread of the European gypsy moth. This destructive insect has a devastating effect on more than 300 varieties of American trees and shrubs. The current regulations prohibit transporting such things as firewood, barbecue grills, outdoor furniture, and mobile homes from infested areas to noninfested areas, since female gypsy moths often attach their egg masses to these objects.

3

In 2009, residents in Cleveland, Ohio, observed the Year of the River by celebrating the recovery of the Cayuhoga River. This river, once *so polluted* that debris floating in the water caught fire and burned on many occasions, is again clean and healthy, thanks to environmental laws and the help of numerous citizens' groups.

4

Since the 19th century, the area that encompasses the southern and central parts of the Appalachian Mountain range in the eastern United States has been referred to as "Appalachia." Populated largely by the descendants of English and Scottish settlers, its present-day residents still speak a distinct dialect of English, and possess their own styles of music, folklore, and Christian worship.

5

Many of the mountain peoples of Laos supported the United States during the Vietnam War. In the late 1970s, many of them settled in the United States, primarily in Minnesota, Wisconsin, Michigan, and California. Although most of them had supported themselves in Southeast Asia by doing very small-scale farming, the majority of these refugees were relocated to relatively large U.S. cities. Most of them did not know how to read and write. As you can imagine, their early years as new Americans were marked by significant obstacles.

6

Lake Havasu City is located west of the Mojave Mountains, on the eastern shore of Lake Havasu – a lake formed by the Parker Dam on the Colorado River to serve as a water reservoir. Its natural setting is characterized by sparse desert vegetation and red rock hills. The city is a carefully laid out mix of residential and commercial areas, and natural spaces. Its most unusual feature is that it is the new home of the London Bridge; when the city of London found it necessary to replace the 136-year-old structure, it was carefully dismantled and reassembled in the Arizona desert.

7

As humans developed, they learned how to make clothing to protect themselves from the elements, how to domesticate animals, how to channel water to irrigate their crops, and how to use fire to heat their living spaces and cook their food. These new skills allowed their numbers to increase.

8

Although the smallpox vaccination was discovered in the late 18th century, it was not until 1967 that the World Health Organization began to implement a plan aimed at wiping out the disease, which was still claiming more than 10 million lives each year. In 1980, the WHO endorsed the medical community's claims that the disease had been eradicated.

Activity C: I'm still confused about …

Professor: So, was everyone able to finish the reading about the five themes of human geography for today? What did you think of it?

Carla: It's really interesting. And it's really cool that we're from so many different places. We're gonna have a lot to compare.

Quentin: That *will* be cool. I've got a question, though.

Professor: What's that, Quentin?

Quentin: While I was reading, I wanted to make really sure I understood those definitions. I was trying to say which of the five themes the photos were illustrating, but according to our book, I got some of them wrong. Like, they had a picture of a six-lane road and a big shopping mall in the part about the "Human-Created Characteristics of Place." Wouldn't you say that was Human-Environment Interaction? What's the difference between the two?

Professor: Good question. The concept of "place" refers to what you see – the "landscape," so to speak. Both the natural characteristics and what humans have added to them. But when you think of the *actions* of humans changing the environment by digging and building things, draining wetlands, and so forth, *then* you're focusing on the actual interaction.

Quentin: Oh. So, you're saying that it depends on what you're emphasizing. That makes sense. Thanks.

Carla: Hey, while we're talking about interaction, I thought of a really good example.

Quentin: Yeah?

Carla: Well, it was easy for me to see how humans change the environment, but I was trying to figure out, "How does the *environment* affect *humans*?" So, I got to thinking about prehistoric humans. When they moved to a new place where the land and the climate were different, they probably had to figure out new ways to survive. And there might have been different plants and animals, too, so they would have had to figure out which ones were safe to eat and hunt. If a poisonous plant killed a caveman, I guess I'd call that a pretty major environmental effect!

Quentin: That's a good example, Carla – funny, too!

Carla: Not so funny if you were the caveman!

Activity M: Fill in the gaps.

1

Medford, Oregon, is just 75 miles east of the Pacific Ocean, but because it lies on the other side of the Siskyou Mountains, it takes more than three hours to drive there. The best way to get there is to go south into northern California, and then to turn north to reach the small towns on the Oregon coast.

2

Minneapolis and St. Paul, Minnesota, are called the Twin Cities, but people often refer to this large urban area simply as "Minneapolis." This annoys the St. Paulites, as they resent having their identity "swallowed up" by the name of their neighbor to the west.

3

American athletes often train in high-altitude cities like Denver, Colorado. Because there's about 17 percent less oxygen at an altitude of 5000 feet above sea level, athletes produce more red blood cells, and thus their metabolisms are raised.

4

New technology has created new ways for people to become victims of kidnapping, stalking, and other sorts of crimes. When posting photos taken by smart cell phones and digital cameras, you may be broadcasting your GPS coordinates to anyone with even a very small amount of technological knowledge. You should always disable the application that transmits this "metadata" about your location before you send any photos.

5

A recent engineering study proposes to block any connection between the Mississippi River and Lake Michigan for fear that invasive fish species like the Asian carp might take over the Great Lakes. The carp are gradually making their way up the Mississippi. If they were to populate Lake Michigan in sufficient numbers, this would eventually choke off other fish, because the carp would consume an enormous amount of the food that those other fish now eat.

6

In the past, many people disposed of their unwanted medications by pouring them down the drain or flushing them down the toilet. But not all water treatment systems were able to clean the medicines out of the water, so they ended up in rivers, lakes and groundwater. This can harm all animals – from fish to humans. Nowadays, most pharmacies and drug companies have programs that take care of this. If you send medicines you're not going to use back to them, they'll dispose of them safely.

Activity N: On your own.

1

Illinois, Indiana, Michigan, Ohio, and Pennsylvania are states in the American Midwest and Northeast whose economies were heavily based on the making of steel, and the manufacturing of products like automobiles. In the 1960s and 1970s, many of the manufacturing jobs moved to the southern U.S. or overseas, and there was also a lesser demand for U.S. steel. These changes led to the abandonment of factories, to higher unemployment rates, and to lower populations in major cities. Because these negative changes were all due to the decay of industries involving steel, a new term was coined to describe this depressed region: the "Rust Belt."

2

Looking down on the city of San Francisco from one of its many hills, you'll see Golden Gate Park in the northern part of the city. It's a rectangular park that's three miles long. It was modeled on New York's Central Park, but it's almost 25 percent larger. Those two main streets that traverse it are named after the late president John F. Kennedy and the Reverend Dr. Martin Luther King, Jr. You can see on this map that the park has many small lakes and ponds, various gardens and sports fields, and lots of green space. In the 1960s it was the site of many so-called "hippie" activities. Since the 1980s, homeless people have begun living in the park. Police and various social activists can't agree on what to do about this situation, and it has made San Franciscans very aware of social problems within their city.

3

The Crazy Horse Memorial is being carved into Thunderhead Mountain in the Black Hills of South Dakota, just 17 miles from Mount Rushmore, where the heads of four famous U.S. presidents were carved into the rock. Crazy Horse was a great warrior from the Oglala Lakota tribe. The sculpture was commissioned in 1929 by a Lakota tribal leader, Henry Standing Bear. He insisted that it be in the Black Hills (even though the rock there isn't great for carving) because that land is considered sacred by many Lakota. Standing Bear explained that he wanted European-Americans to know that Native Americans had heroes, too.

4

In the 18th century, before the American Revolution, the British began to gain power along the Atlantic coast of North America. The French settlers living in the area in the Northeast called Acadia (that's A-C-A-D-I-A) resisted them. The British expelled many of those French rebels during and after the French and Indian War (1754–1763). They eventually migrated south, and settled in the French-colonized part of America that is now the state of Louisiana. At that point, their name, "Acadian" morphed into the name "Cajun" (C-A-J-U-N), a name by which they're still known today. In 1980, they were officially recognized by the U.S. federal government as a distinct ethnic group.

Activity V: The rural exodus.

We've been talking about the ways in which people must adapt in order to live in different environments. One kind of "adaptation" we haven't mentioned, though, is adapting by *moving away* from that environment, and finding new places to live and new ways of living. Let me give you an example: the case of sub-Saharan Africa. Because of severe droughts, the difficulty of acquiring farmland, and the falling prices of agricultural products in global markets, it's getting harder and harder for some Africans to make a living as small farmers, and there aren't many other kinds of jobs available in rural areas. In addition, many rural areas don't have electricity, water, or other amenities of cities, like shops, movie theaters, and restaurants. Access to education and health care is often limited as well. Studies show that all of these factors encourage young people – especially young men – to leave the countryside in search of a better life.

The trouble is, they often arrive in the city without much cash for food and rent, and with no job skills. As more and more of them arrive in cities, the government has to spend more money on water and sewers, public transportation, and the like. This prevents it from carrying out much-needed development projects in rural areas. In addition, even as unemployment rates, crime rates, and drug use rise in cities, rural areas are beginning to suffer from a lack of agricultural workers and a decrease in the fertility of the farmland.

Researchers believe that within the next 20 years, more than 50 percent of the populations of many African countries will be living in cities, and the cities simply can't accommodate this many people. Statistics show that more than two thirds of the city dwellers in sub-Saharan Africa already live in slums. They live in small, poorly built houses constructed with discarded pieces of wood, metal, cardboard, and plastic. Slum-dwellers often have access to water that they can carry to their homes, but most slums don't have sewers; human and animal waste often flow through trenches that run down the middle of the settlements' dirt roads.

An example of such a slum is Kibera, located about five miles from the center of Nairobi, Kenya. Kibera is estimated to be the third largest slum in the world, with a population nearing 300,000. For years, the Kenyan government has been trying to find ways to upgrade the living conditions in Kibera and to help residents relocate to other places in the city or encourage them to return to the rural areas. However, each of these possible strategies is complicated by many human, logistical, and political issues.

CHAPTER 7

Activity B: You should apply!

1

Nick: Why does that job interest you?

Betty: Because I'd really love not being cooped up in an office all day. And it looks like I could still be home every night.

Nick: Are you going to apply?

Betty: Well, I don't have my commercial driver's license yet. But some day …

2

Daria: A server's job? You can't be serious!

Erik: You don't get it, do you? This isn't a temporary job; it's a career. Lots of people stay in a job like this for their whole working life. The work environment is really nice, and the tips are amazing. When I have some more experience, this is the kind of job I want to have.

3

Meghan: Who knew that taking care of Aunt Beth for all those years was a job experience? Did you see this ad?

Steve: Yeah, it looks as though the salary is actually decent, too.

Meghan: Yes, it does. I guess I'd better start saving for a car …

4

Barry: Are you going to apply for that management job?

Sun-yi: I dunno.

Barry: You've got the degree in econ, so you might as well.

Sun-yi: Yeah, but I think I'd like to start with something that's more hands on. I think I'll skip it.

5

Jenn: Wow, check this one out. I could totally do this!

Cesar: Hey, yeah, and you even speak Spanish! How great is that?

Jenn: Mmm hmmm.

Cesar: I thought you liked your job, though.

Jenn: Yeah, well … I really like the people I work with, but after four years, I'm ready to move on. I'm actually kinda bored. I'd like to get into something more challenging where I also have more to do.

6

Cathy: Do you think there's any point in applying? I was a *theater major*!

Roy: Of course there is! You worked on the sets and costumes for every play you were in, and some of it was children's theater. Duh …

Cathy: You're right! I can't think of anything I'd rather do. And really, what have I got to lose?

7

Mitch: I just have a feeling this one pays more than the job I'm in now.

Shae: So, are you gonna go for it?

Mitch: I guess not. I really prefer working for a small firm. And besides, I've never done it, but tax law sounds boring, and litigation sounds too stressful.

Activity C: Career Counseling.

Bill: Hello, – Ms. Lee, is it?

Janice: Yes, that's right.

Bill: Hi, I'm Bill. Let's take a look at your resume. Hmm …. OK. For a first draft, this is pretty good, actually. I just have a few suggestions. First, when did you graduate from Emancipation?

Janice: I'm still going there. I'll graduate in June.

Bill: OK, after "2012," you should add a hyphen, and then the word "present." That means you're still there. And then you put "ADN" – associate's degree in nursing, is that right?

Janice: Correct.

Bill: "ADN expected Spring 2013." Good. Now, under **Objectives**, what you have is fine, but it might sound more professional if you said "To obtain an entry-level pediatric nursing position, including parent education." Does that make sense?

Janice: Yes, it sounds good. Um, I have a question. Under **Work Experience**? I know you're supposed to say what you did in a job, but I don't really know what to say about a restaurant job. Is what I have OK like that?

Bill: Hmm. Ideally, you should try to connect it to the job you want in some way. How about "Provided prompt and courteous service to … blah, blah, blah, in a fast-paced environment." That suggests you have people skills, and that you work well under pressure.

Janice: OK.

Bill: Now, just a couple more things. For both your café and your intern jobs, why don't you say "physicians" instead of "doctors." It just sounds a little more formal. And, instead of "health-care workers," put "health-care professionals." For the same reason.

Janice: Sure, fine. Thanks.

Bill: And then, instead of "and giving vaccination shots," you could put either " … with well-baby visits and 'vaccinations'," or " … well-baby visits and 'immunizations'." Did you get all of that?

Janice: Yes, I think so.

Bill: Oh, one more thing. You want your resume to fill one neat page. So, you might want to list your skills on three separate lines, just to make it look nicer on the page …

Janice: Thanks so much. It sounds a lot better!

Activity K: Take a guess!

1

Hostess: Good evening. How are you all doing tonight? Do you have a reservation?

Boris: Yes, we've got a reservation for three under the name of Sercovich.

Hostess: Excellent. Let me show you to your table.

2

Michelle: Good evening, I'm Michelle and I'm going to be your server tonight.

Boris: Great.

Michelle: I'll be right back with the menus.

Boris: Sorry? With what?

Michelle: The menus.

3

Michelle: Could I start you all out with something to drink? And maybe some appetizers?

Boris: Could we have some sparkling mineral water, please?

Michelle: I'll get your water right away. And … any appetizers?

Boris: Excuse me? The …?

Michelle: Appetizers. Here's a list of what we have, right here at the top of the menu.

Boris: Thanks. We'll take a look.

4

Michelle: I hope everything was to your liking. Are you ready for some dessert?

Boris: Yes, I'll take care of it. I assume you accept most types of credit cards?

Michelle: Sorry. I was asking about dessert. We have fruit tarts, chocolate cake, and house-made ice creams and sorbets.

Boris: Oh, of course. Who'd like something?

5

Michelle: And how about some coffee? We have regular coffee, decaf, and espresso drinks.

Boris: I'll just have a regular coffee, please. How about the rest of you? Three coffees, please.

Michelle: And would anyone like cream?

Boris: I'm sorry, could you repeat that?

Michelle: Pardon me. I was asking whether anyone wanted cream with the coffee.

Boris: Uh …

Michelle: Cream? Or milk?

Boris: Oh, thanks. I'll just have mine black. Katie and Andrew, what about you?

Activity L: You're hired!

Mrs. Walker: Hi, Ms. Sanchez, I hope you had a good interview with Mr. Adams.

Ms. Sanchez: Yes, I did. It was very informative.

Mrs. Walker: He tells me that you seem inclined to accept our offer. Let's talk a bit more so that I can get to know you.

Ms. Sanchez: Yes, I'd like that.

Mrs. Walker: OK. Then you can give me your Social Security number and we'll be all set.

Ms. Sanchez: Umm. That's fine.

Mrs. Walker: Hey, I see you went to Emancipation Community College. How long ago was it that you got your diploma?

Ms. Sanchez: Let's see. Um, I went there for 18 months, I finished about two years ago, and I got my LPN license last summer.

Mrs. Walker: Great, congratulations! … So, as you know, your primary responsibilities will be helping your clients bathe and dress, doing some simple meal preparation – both for lunch while you're there, and then something for them to have for dinner – and then doing some light housekeeping. You might do the dishes, sweep the floors, change the sheets on the bed, do a little laundry, straighten up the living room – things like that. Nothing major. Just relieve our clients of some of those little tasks that can seem difficult when they don't have much energy.

Ms. Sanchez: Yes, I think Mr. Adams explained all of that. Basically, I'll help them take a bath or shower, make them some lunch and make sure there's something in the fridge for dinner, and maybe do the dishes or clean up a little bit?

Mrs. Walker: Precisely. Well, I think that's about all, Ms. Sanchez. Um, do you have any other questions for me?

Ms. Sanchez: Just one. Mr. Adams wasn't quite sure what my salary would be. Can you tell me what your hourly rate is?

Mrs. Walker: Gladly. We pay an hourly rate of ten fifty. You should know that's about 20 percent more than other agencies in the city. You'll also be eligible for a 10 percent raise after the first year if you have good evaluations.

Ms. Sanchez: Uh …

Mrs. Walker: I'll put the exact figures in an e-mail to confirm this.

Ms. Sanchez: Great, that'll help me a lot.

Mrs. Walker: All right! I just need your Social Security number, and then we'll be all set.

Ms. Sanchez: I'm sorry. What do you need?

Mrs. Walker: Your Social Security number. You can just fill it in on these forms.

Ms. Sanchez: Oh, right! Perfect.

Mrs. Walker: Well, it's certainly been a pleasure to chat with you. And I really hope that you'll accept our offer. I think you'd enjoy working here.

Ms. Sanchez: Thanks very much for your time, Mrs. Walker.

Activity U: On the one hand …

Fatima: Professor Conley, I've got a decision to make, and I don't know what to do.

Prof. Conley: Well, why don't you tell me what's going on?

Fatima: OK, so you know I've been working on a teaching certificate.

Prof. Conley: Yes … and I've always thought that you were really committed to that idea.

Fatima: Well, I *was*. I *am*!

Prof. Conley: So?

Fatima: Well, I've been in school for a little more than four years at this point, and I've still got so many courses

to take. It will take me at least one more year – maybe even almost two – to finish.

Prof. Conley: Well, it's true that there are a lot of required courses for getting certified. But I thought you were enjoying most of them.

Fatima: Yeah, I am. It's not that I don't like them – it's just the time it's taking, and the money I'm borrowing to get through school …

Prof. Conley: Hmm. Tell me, where are these second thoughts coming from?

Fatima: My best friend's father has a small business, and he's offered me a full-time job with great benefits.

Prof. Conley: Oh, I see.

Fatima: I'd be a buyer, so I'd get to travel as part of the job. I've gotta tell you – it sounds really interesting.

Prof. Conley: Yes, it does. Tell me, Fatima, where do you see yourself in 10 years?

Fatima: Well, I've always *figured* that I'd be teaching little kids somewhere …

Prof. Conley: So, here's where we are, I guess. On the one hand, an interesting job right now with a good salary, and on the other hand, a year or so more of school, the job you've been preparing for, and a little more debt.

Fatima: Hmm, that makes it sound easy. Who would be crazy enough to turn down a sure thing to spend two more years in school?

Prof. Conley: Somebody who loves teaching, maybe?

Fatima: I really love working with little kids …

Prof. Conley: That sounds like a decision to me …

Fatima: Yeah, but I've been really anxious about the future lately. What if I spend two more years studying, and then can't get a job?

Prof. Conley: I don't think there's too much danger of that, frankly. With the letters of recommendation you'll get from your professors, I'm guessing you'll be just fine.

Fatima: Really? Thanks! So maybe …

Prof. Conley: You know, there is another possibility. You're still pretty young. You could take the job for a few years, and then, if you're not enjoying it, you could always go back to school.

Fatima: True. You know what? I just made up my mind. I'm gonna stay in school.

Prof. Conley: Really! I thought you were leaning the other way.

Fatima: Well, I was. But, you know, teaching is just more interesting to me. It's way better than a job as a buyer. If I know this is really what I want, I should just go for it. Who knows, my life might get a lot more complicated in the next few years. And when you travel for business, I'm guessing, it's not all that much fun.

Prof. Conley: Well then! … I just love this job. As your wise, old advisor, all I did was sit here while you made your own decision!

Fatima: That's not true. It always helps me to talk with you.

CHAPTER 8

Activity B: Every place is unique.

1

We used to go there every Sunday afternoon to get ice cream. Then we'd walk over to the school playground to eat it and play on the swings. It was so peaceful – the only sound you heard was children laughing.

2

Yeah, it is a bit noisy. Especially since we live around the corner from the fire station. Even so – and you might think I'm crazy – I love it. And my favorite bakery is just next door. I'm in heaven.

3

We moved here about five years ago. I hated it because it seemed too quiet. It was too small, and there weren't any big stores. Then I started meeting my neighbors and going to a book discussion group at the public library. That's when things started getting better.

4

There's a really modern community center where they put on plays and concerts, and a lot of clubs meet there too. It's great. It keeps the kids busy and they're really proud of what they accomplish.

5

This area had a really colorful past. It was a notorious hangout for gangsters in the 1920s. That little shop over there was the restaurant where they always ate and did business. It had two secret exits so they could get away from the cops if there was a raid. Who knew?

6

I love my neighbors. We're all so different, but we all get along. Now that we've cleaned up the park together, we have a very united community. In the summer, we have informal barbecues; people just show up and share whatever they've got. Then we play softball. We're all pretty bad, but we have *such* a good time …

7

Anyone who visits our neighborhood might think it's unfriendly, but I don't think that's it. Most of the residents are professionals who work many hours, and after long days, nobody has the energy to get to know their neighbors all that well. We say "hi" when we see each other in the coffee shop or the bookstore, but when we get home from work, everyone wants to be alone and chill out. I think it's because our jobs involve so much interaction with people.

8

When I was a kid, that plaza was full of "hippies." They didn't camp there like the Occupy Wall Street people did, but on the weekends, that place was crowded. They all had long hair, and they played guitars and sang songs about peace. My folks thought they were really naïve, but I think they *did* change the world a little bit, don't you?

Activity C: Welcome to the neighborhood!

Joan: Oh, hello!

Carolina: Hi, we just wanted to stop by and introduce ourselves. We're your next-door neighbors, the Godoys. I'm Carolina, and this is Tony.

Joan: Would you like to come in for a few minutes? We were just going to take a break, and I have some iced tea all ready.

Tony: Sure, that'd be great. But we won't stay long. I'm sure you've got a lot of unpacking to do.

Tony: So, California, huh? What brings you to Minneapolis?

Bill: Joan's accounting firm has offices here, and they transferred her to be the director of this branch. We were just fine with moving, too. The weather in California is great, but everything is so expensive there. We got this house for half the price of our old one, and this one is a lot bigger.

Tony: What about you, Bill? What do you do?

Bill: Well, I was an art director for a big advertising company, but I got laid off last spring, and I've been a stay-at-home dad ever since. We're really enjoying the lifestyle of having one person keep the family organized. I'm going to work freelance, but I may not go back to full time until our daughters are in high school. How about you two?

Carolina: I'm a nurse, and Tony teaches second grade at the school your kids'll be going to. I'm sure you'll like it here.

Joan: We fell in love with it the first time we saw it. We both grew up in neighborhoods like this. I love the big old houses, and the girls can walk to school *and* the library.

Bill: We'll just see how much *I* love big old houses by the time I finish fixing it up. There's a lot of work to do.

Carolina: Tell us about it! Our house was pretty rundown, too. We're not handy, so we paid to have ours fixed up. We'd save up enough money to do one room, and then we'd save again 'til we could do the next ... It took us five years. The workmen who did it are practically like family now.

Bill: So, what's the history of the neighborhood?

Tony: Well, originally, this was a pretty high-class neighborhood. The people who lived here had made their fortunes in stuff like railroads, milling, and lumber. When they moved on, the college professors who taught at St. Elizabeth's moved in. Then St. E's closed, but at least they were able to turn those beautiful old buildings into a high school.

Carolina: So, as the profs moved away, most of these houses were rented out. That's when they started to be a little neglected.

Tony: But now lots of young families have bought up the houses, and we really have a sense of community. We have block parties and barbecues, and *almost* everyone participates.

Carolina: I'll tell you more about *that* later ...

Tony: Yeah, save the gossip for another time. We should get going, Caro, and let these folks get back to work.

Joan: Hey, thanks for stopping by!

Activity L: I suspect that …

1

Brian: Hi, Professor Romero. I'm going to be in your advanced conversation class next semester!

Carmen: Oh. This course is a lot more difficult than the last one you took with me. I'm going to send you a syllabus right away so you can look it over.

2

Ramón: Wanna get together and play racquetball tonight?

Phil: Actually, let's make it next week. Maybe both Tuesday and Thursday? My wife's parents're coming to stay with us for 10 days, and they'll be here by then.

3

Cathy: Peter just asked me out on a date.

Jen: Be careful. I predict that he'll go out with you for a while, and really make you think he likes you, and then he'll drop you and never speak to you again.

4

Randall: Wow, I just heard that Alan is leaving the company.

Harriet: Yes, and *most* people don't know the real story …

5

Ahmed: Today we're going to work in teams.

Stephen: Um … I wouldn't mind being assigned to the boss's group. We haven't had the chance to get to know each other very well yet. I'd like him to know who I am …

6

Ron: Hi, sorry it took me a while to get back to you. What's up? Is something wrong?

Portia: Oh, no, not really. Um … I've just been thinking it would be interesting to see a psychologist sometime. You know the names of a couple of good people, don't you?

7

Bursar: Yes, sir, you had a question?

Brent: Yes, I was wondering if there's any flexibility around the date when my spring tuition is due.

8

Dr. Fritz: So, Dr. Caldwell, as you know, we'll be having you teach some sample classes and meet with all the members of our department individually.

Dr. Caldwell: Yes, I understand. I'm looking forward to it.

Dr. Fritz: Well, I, uh … I just wanted to tell you that if someone says something to you that surprises or upsets you, I'd ask you to please come and tell me about it right away.

Activity M: Reading between the lines.

Joan: Cookies! You really didn't have to do that. And thanks for the coffee!

Carolina: Well, I thought you needed a little treat. Unpacking is no fun. You seem to be making real progress, though.

Joan: Yes, I've found that the sooner you get the public areas of the house presentable, the better you feel.

Carolina: Well, hang in there. It's looking good. When do you start work?

Joan: On Monday. It'll be a challenge … Their last director left rather suddenly, and most of the employees liked him a lot. I'm not able to explain much about it to them, so I hope everything goes OK.

Carolina: I'm sure it'll be fine. Hey, I meant to say that your daughters are delightful. Are they twins?

Joan: No, and once you get to know them, you'll see that they couldn't be more different. Ellen gets straight A's in school, and always has her nose in a book. Pat is, uh, she's our star athlete. She's been playing soccer since she was four. Her dream is to play on the U.S. Olympic team, and I could actually see that happening! Do the kids play soccer in the elementary school here?

Carolina: Uh … I *think* so … And then there's a soccer club …

Joan: Oh, great. Is it near here?

Carolina: Not *too* far.

Joan: Where exactly is it?

Carolina: You just go down to the end of West Main St., and you take a right onto Berkeley St. When you get to the bottom of the hill, you'll see the parking lot on your right.

Joan: Thanks – we'll check it out right away. When Pat's not getting enough exercise, we all suffer.

Carolina: So, have you done any exploring yet?

Joan: Not much. We did find the bakery over on Mill St.

Carolina: Oh, good. You know, though, there's another one you might like even better, and you can walk there.

Joan: Oh, really? And where is that one?

Carolina: If you go out your *back* door and down the alley, you turn right on Cedar, and it's two blocks down, on the left. I like it because the owners are really friendly, they never sell bread from the day before without telling you, and you always get great service. Once I forgot to pick up Rosario's birthday cake, and they actually stopped by and *delivered* it on their way home after they closed. I'd go there, if I were you.

Joan: I'm sold. Say, there was something I wanted to ask you.

Carolina: Yes?

Joan: Yesterday you said that *most* of the neighbors were friendly and socialized together. I don't want to gossip, but is there anything I should know about that?

Carolina: I guess I was talking about Mrs. Bartlett. She's rather standoffish. She's older, and she may have some health problems, so maybe that's why she can be a little bit mean. Some of our neighbors are really upset about it. Frankly, I can accept the fact that she doesn't want to go to any of the neighbors' parties. What does bother me, though, is that she's called the police a couple of times when there was a loud party or when someone's dog ran into her yard. She never talks directly to her neighbors about these things, and that's too bad.

Joan: Thanks for telling me. Of course, I plan to be friendly with everyone in the neighborhood, but if she seems unfriendly to us, I won't let it hurt my feelings.

Activity V: Let's do lunch!

Karl: … So, you're in Chicago now! Where are you living?

Andre: Well, they've put me in a company-owned high-rise apartment with a view of Lake Michigan. It's pretty impressive. This may be the only time I ever experience luxury living, so I'm trying not to get used to it.

Karl: So you're right downtown? That's great!

Andre: Mm-hm. But you know, I wouldn't really want to live here permanently, even if I were really rich.

Karl: Why is that?

Andre: Well, I feel as though I'm staying in a hotel. Completely anonymous. I never even *see* the other people who live here, although I *know* there must *be* some. It's so quiet that I feel like I should whisper all the time. And I'm several blocks away from any green space. Luckily there are a few plants here, so I know I'm not in a spaceship on my way to Mars.

Karl: Come on, they say Chicago's an amazing city!

Andre: Yeah, you're right. I'm close to Symphony Hall, and the Art Institute, and other cultural stuff. But at night, unless you're in a shopping area, or by a theater or something, it feels pretty empty. And the shops are all pretty fancy. There aren't that many places to buy groceries, or ordinary kitchen stuff, or a hammer and nails …

Karl: Why would you want a hammer and nails?

Andre: Well, I wouldn't, but you know what I mean.

Karl: Yeah, sorry. Hey, the reason I'm calling is that I'm actually going to be in Chicago on business for the next couple of days, and I was hoping we could get together. I'll be at the Palmer House hotel downtown.

Andre: Oh wow, that's right near my office! It'd be great to see you. Would you be available for lunch tomorrow?

Karl: Yes, I think so. My plane gets in at around 10:00. I don't really like taking taxis, though. Have you figured out the public transportation system yet?

Andre: Of course I have! Have you got a pencil?

Karl: Uh huh. Ready.

Andre: OK, what terminal are you arriving at?

Karl: Terminal 2, I think.

Andre: OK, when you get off the plane, look for a walkway that will take you to the main parking garage. There you'll find the CTA station – that's Chicago Transit Authority, but you don't care about that. Anyway, you take the Blue Line towards the Loop – that's what they call downtown Chicago. It'll only cost you a couple of bucks, and it should take you less than an hour to get here.

Karl: OK, then what?

Andre: Get off at the Monroe/Dearborn stop. Walk east down Monroe St. toward Michigan Avenue – that's one of the main downtown streets – anyone can point you in that direction. Just walk about a half a block and the hotel is on your right. You can drop your stuff off there first. Then, if you walk another block and a half, you'll see that you're practically across the street from Millennium Park. I can meet you at a restaurant there called Park Grill. Should we say a little before noon?

Karl: Perfect. I'll call you if I'm delayed, but if you don't hear from me, that means all is well. I'm really looking forward to seeing you.

Speaker's Handbook

1. Greetings, Introductions, and Leave-taking

Greeting someone you know

Hello.
Hi.
Hey.
Morning.
How's it going? *(informal)*
What's up? *(informal)*

Greeting someone you haven't seen for a while

It's good to see you again.
It's been a long time.
How long has it been?
Long time no see! *(informal)*
You look great! *(informal)*
So what have you been up to? *(informal)*

Greeting someone you don't know

Hello.
Good morning.
Good afternoon.
Good evening.
Hi, there! *(informal)*

Saying goodbye

Goodbye.
Bye.
Bye-bye.
See you.
See you later.
Have a good day.
Take care.
Good night. *(only when saying goodbye)*

Introducing yourself

Hi, I'm Tom.
Hello, my name is Tom.
Excuse me.
We haven't met.
My name is Tom. *(formal)*

I saw you in (science) class.
I met you at Jane's party.

Introducing other people

Have you two met?
Have you met Maria?
I'd like you to meet Maria.
There's someone I'd like you to meet.
Let me introduce you to Maria.
   You: This is my friend Maria.
   Ali: Glad to meet you, Maria.
   You: Maria, this is Ali.
   Maria: Nice to meet you, Ali.
I've been wanting to meet you.
Tom has told me a lot about you.

Greeting guests

Welcome.
Oh, hi.
How are you?
Please come in.
Glad you could make it.
Did you have any trouble finding us?
Can I take your coat?
Have a seat.
Please make yourself at home.
   You: Can I get you something to drink?
   Guest: Yes, please.
   You: What would you like?
   Guest: I'll have some orange juice.
What can I get you to drink?
Would you like some . . . ?

Saying goodbye to guests

Thanks for coming.
Thanks for joining us.
I'm so glad you could come.
It wouldn't have been the same
   without you.
Let me get your things.
Stop by anytime.

2. Having a Conversation

Starting a conversation
Nice weather, huh?
Aren't you a friend of Jim's?
Did you see last night's game?
What's your favorite TV show?
So, what do you think about (the situation in Europe)?
So, how do you like (your new car)?
Guess what I did last night?

Showing that you are listening
Uh-huh.
Right.
Exactly.
Yeah.
OK . . .
I know what you mean.

Giving yourself time to think
Well . . .
Um . . .
Uh . . .
Let me think.
Just a minute.
> **Other:** We should ride our bikes.
> **You:** It's too far. And, I mean . . . , it's raining and we're already late.

Checking for comprehension
Do you see what I mean?
Are you with me?
Does that make sense?

Checking for agreement
Don't you agree?
So what do you think?
We have to (act fast), you know?

Expressing agreement
You're right.
I couldn't agree with you more.
Good thinking! (informal)
You said it! (informal)
You're absolutely right.
Absolutely! (informal)

Expressing disagreement
I'm afraid I disagree.
Yeah, but . . .
I see your point, but . . .
That's not true.

You must be joking! (informal)
No way! (informal)

Asking someone to repeat something
Excuse me?
Sorry?
I didn't quite get that.
Could you repeat that?
Could you say that again?
Say again? (informal)

Interrupting someone
Excuse me.
Yes, but (we don't have enough time).
I know, but (that will take hours).
Wait a minute. (informal)
Just hold it right there! (impolite)

Changing the topic
By the way, what do you think about (the new teacher)?
Before I forget, (there's a free concert on Friday night).
Whatever . . . (Did you see David's new car?)
Enough about me. Let's talk about you.

Ending a conversation
It was nice talking with you.
Good seeing you.
Sorry, I have to go now.

3. Using the Telephone

Making personal calls
Hi, this is David.
Is this Alice?
Is Alice there?
May I speak with Alice, please? (formal)
I work with her.
We're in the same science class.
Could you tell her I called?
Would you ask her to call me?

Answering personal calls
Hello?
Who's calling, please?
Oh, hi, David. How are you?
I can't hear you.
Sorry, we got cut off.
I'm in the middle of something.
Can I call you back?
What's your number again?
Listen. I have to go now.
It was nice talking to you.

Answering machine greetings

You've reached 212-555-6701.
Please leave a message after the beep.
Hi, this is Carlos.
I can't take your call right now.
Sorry I missed your call.
Please leave your name and number.
I'll call you back as soon as I can.

Answering machine messages

This is Magda. Call me back when you
    get a chance. *(informal)*
Call me back on my cell.
I'll call you back later.
Talk to you later.
If you get this message before 11:00, please
    call me back.

Making business calls

Hello. This is Andy Larson.
I'm calling about . . .
Is this an OK time?

Answering business calls

Apex Electronics. Rosa Baker speaking. *(formal)*
Hello, Rosa Baker.
May I help you?
Who's calling, please?

> **Caller:** May I speak with Mr. Hafner, please?
> **Businessperson:** This is he.

> **Caller:** Mr. Hafner, please.
> **Businessperson:** Speaking.

Talking to an office assistant

Extension 716, please.
Customer Service, please.
May I speak with Sheila Spink, please?
She's expecting my call.
I'm returning her call.
I'd like to leave a message for Ms. Spink.

Making appointments on the phone

> **You:** I'd like to make an appointment to see Ms. Spink.
> **Assistant:** How's 11:00 on Wednesday?
> **You:** Wednesday is really bad for me.
> **Assistant:** Can you make it Thursday at 9:00?
> **You:** That would be perfect!
> **Assistant:** OK. I have you down for Thursday at 9:00.

Special explanations

I'm sorry. She's not available.
Is there something I can help you with?
Can I put you on hold?
I'll transfer you to that extension.
If you leave your number, I'll have Ms. Spink call
    you back.
I'll tell her you called.

4. Interviewing for a Job

Small talk by the interviewer

Thanks for coming in today.
Did you have any trouble finding us?
How was the drive?
Would you like a cup of coffee?
Do you happen to know (Terry Mendham)?

Small talk by the candidate

What a great view!
Thanks for arranging to see me.
I've been looking forward to meeting you.
I spent some time exploring the company's website.
My friend, Dale, has worked here for
    several years.

Getting serious

OK, shall we get started?
So, anyway . . .
Let's get down to business.

General questions for a candidate

Tell me a little about yourself.
How did you get into this line of work?
How long have you been in this country?
How did you learn about the opening?
What do you know about this company?
Why are you interested in working for us?

General answers to an interviewer

I've always been interested in (finance).
I enjoy (working with numbers).
My (uncle) was (an accountant) and encouraged me to
    try it.
I saw your ad in the paper.
This company has a great reputation in the field.

Job-related questions for a candidate

What are your qualifications for this job?

Describe your work experience.

What were your responsibilities on your last job?

I'd like to hear more about (your supervisory experience).

> **Interviewer:** Have you taken any courses in (bookkeeping)?
>
> **You:** Yes, I took two courses in business school and another online course last year.

What interests you about this particular job?

Why do you think it's a good fit?

Why did you leave your last job?

Do you have any experience with (HTML)?

Would you be willing to (travel eight weeks a year)?

What sort of salary are you looking for?

Describing job qualifications to an interviewer

In (2000), I started working for (Booker's) as a (sales rep).

After (two years), I was promoted to (sales manager).

You'll notice on my resume that (I supervised six people).

I was responsible for (three territories).

I was in charge of (planning sales meetings).

I have experience in all areas of (sales).

I helped implement (online sales reports).

I had to (contact my reps) on a daily basis.

I speak (Spanish) fluently.

I think my strong points are (organization and punctuality).

Ending the interview

I'm impressed with your experience.

I'd like to arrange a second interview.

When would you be able to start?

You'll hear from us by (next Wednesday).

We'll be in touch.

5. Agreeing and Disagreeing

Agreeing

Yeah, that's right.

I know it.

I agree with you.

You're right.

That's true.

I think so, too.

That's what I think.

Me, too.

Me neither.

Agreeing strongly

You're absolutely right!

Definitely!

Certainly!

Exactly!

Absolutely!

Of course!

I couldn't agree more.

You're telling me! *(informal)*

You said it! *(informal)*

Agreeing weakly

I suppose so.

Yeah, I guess so.

It would seem that way.

Remaining neutral

I see your point.

You have a point there.

I understand what you're saying.

I see what you mean.

I'd have to think about that.

I've never thought about it that way before.

Maybe yes, maybe no.

Could be.

Disagreeing

No, I don't think so.

I agree up to a point.

I really don't see it that way.

That's not what I think.

I agree that (going by car is faster), but . . .

But what about (the expense involved)?

Yes, but . . .

I know, but . . .

No, it wasn't. / No, they don't. / *etc.*

> **Other person:** We could save a lot of money by taking the bus.
>
> **You:** Not really. It would cost almost the same as driving.

Disagreeing strongly

I disagree completely.

That's not true.

That is not an option.

Definitely not!

Absolutely not!

You've made your point, but . . .

No way! *(informal)*

You can't be serious. *(informal)*

You've got to be kidding! *(informal)*

Where did you get that idea? *(impolite)*

Are you out of your mind! *(impolite)*

Disagreeing politely

I'm afraid I have to disagree with you.

I'm not so sure.

I'm not sure that's such a good idea.

I see what you're saying, but . . .

I'm sure many people feel that way, but . . .

But don't you think we should consider (other alternatives)?

6. Interrupting, Clarifying, Checking for Understanding

Informal interruptions

Um.

Sir? / Ma'am?

Just a minute.

Can I stop you for a minute?

Wait a minute! *(impolite)*

Hold it right there! *(impolite)*

Formal interruptions

Excuse me, sir / ma'am.

Excuse me for interrupting.

Forgive me for interrupting you, but . . .

I'm sorry to break in like this, but . . .

Could I interrupt you for a minute?

Could I ask a question, please?

Asking for clarification—Informal

What did you say?

I didn't catch that.

Sorry, I didn't get that.

I missed that.

Could you repeat that?

Could you say that again?

Say again?

I'm lost.

Could you run that by me one more time?

Did you say . . . ?

Do you mean . . . ?

Asking for clarification—Formal

I beg your pardon?

I'm not sure I understand what you're saying.

I can't make sense of what you just said.

Could you explain that in different words?

Could you please repeat that?

Could you go over that again?

Giving clarification—Informal

I'll go over it again.

I'll take it step-by-step.

I'll take a different tack this time.

Stop me if you get lost.

OK, here's a recap.

Maybe this will clarify things.

To put it another way, . . .

In other words, . . .

Giving clarification—Formal

Let me put it another way.

Let me give you some examples.

Here are the main points again.

I'm afraid you didn't understand what I said.

I'm afraid you've missed the point.

What I meant was . . .

I hope you didn't think that . . .

I didn't mean to imply that . . .

I hope that clears things up.

Checking for understanding

Do you understand now?

Is it clearer now?

Do you see what I'm getting at?

Does that help?

Is there anything that still isn't clear?

What other questions do you have?

> **Speaker:** What else?
>
> **Listener:** I'm still not clear on the difference between a preposition and a conjunction.

Now explain it to me in your own words.

7. Apologizing

Apologizing for a small accident or mistake
Sorry.
I'm sorry.
Excuse me.
It was an accident.
Pardon me. *(formal)*
Oops! *(informal)*
My mistake. *(informal)*
I'm terrible with (names).
I've never been good with (numbers).
I can't believe I (did) that.

Apologizing for a serious accident or mistake
I'm so sorry.
I am really sorry that I (damaged your car).
I am so sorry about (damaging your car).
I feel terrible about (the accident).
I'm really sorry, but (I was being very careful).
I'm sorry for (causing you a problem).
Please accept my apologies for . . . *(formal)*
I sincerely apologize for . . . *(formal)*

Apologizing for upsetting someone
I'm sorry I upset you.
I didn't mean to make you feel bad.
Please forgive me. *(formal)*
I just wasn't thinking straight.
That's not what I meant to say.
I didn't mean it personally.
I'm sorry. I'm having a rough day.

Apologizing for having to say *no*
I'm sorry. I can't.
Sorry, I never (lend anyone my car).
I wish I could say *yes.*
I'm going to have to say *no.*
I can't. I have to (work that evening).
Maybe some other time.

Responding to an apology
Don't worry about it.
Oh, that's OK.
Think nothing of it. *(formal)*
Don't mention it. *(formal)*
> **Other person:** I'm afraid I lost the pen you lent me.
> **You:** No big thing.
It doesn't matter.
It's not important.

Never mind.
No problem.
It happens.
Forget it.
Don't sweat it. *(informal)*
Apology accepted. *(formal)*

Showing regret
I feel really bad.
It won't happen again.
I wish I could go back and start all over again.
I don't know what came over me.
I don't know what to say.
Now I know better.
Too bad I didn't . . .
It was inexcusable of me. *(formal)*
It's not like me to . . .
I hope I can make it up to you.
That didn't come out right.
I didn't mean to take it out on you.

Sympathizing
This must be very difficult for you.
I know what you mean.
I know how you're feeling.
I know how upset you must be.
I can imagine how difficult this is for you.

8. Suggestions, Advice, Insistence

Making informal suggestions
Here's what I suggest.
I know what you should do.
Why don't you (go to the movies with Jane)?
What about (having lunch with Bob)?
Try (the French fries next time).
Have you thought about (riding your bike to work)?

Accepting suggestions
Thanks, I'll do that.
Good idea!
That's a great idea.
Sounds good to me.
That's a plan.
I'll give it a try.
Guess it's worth a try.

Refusing suggestions

No. I don't like (French fries).

That's not for me.

I don't think so.

That might work for some people, but . . .

Nawww. *(informal)*

I don't feel like it. *(impolite)*

Giving serious advice—Informal

Listen!

Here's the plan.

Take my advice.

Take it from one who knows.

Take it from someone who's been there.

Here's what I think you should do.

Hey! Here's an idea.

How about (waiting until you're 30 to get married)?

Don't (settle down too quickly).

Why don't you (see the world while you're young)?

You can always (settle down later).

Don't forget—(you only live once).

Giving serious advice—Formal

Have you ever thought about (becoming a doctor)?

Maybe it would be a good idea if you (went back to school).

It looks to me like (Harvard) would be your best choice.

If I were you, I'd (study medicine).

In my opinion, you should (consider it seriously).

Be sure to (get your application in early).

I always advise people to (check that it was received).

The best idea is (to study hard).

If you're really smart, you'll (start right away).

Accepting advice

You're right.

Thanks for the advice.

That makes a lot of sense.

I see what you mean.

That sounds like good advice.

I'll give it a try.

I'll do my best.

You've given me something to think about.

I'll try it and get back to you.

Refusing advice

I don't think that would work for me.

That doesn't make sense to me.

I'm not sure that would be such a good idea.

I could never (become a doctor).

Thanks for the input.

Thanks, but no thanks. *(informal)*

You don't know what you're talking about. *(impolite)*

I think I know what's best for myself. *(impolite)*

Back off! *(impolite)*

Insisting

You have to (become a doctor).

Try to see it my way.

I know what I'm talking about.

If you don't (go to medical school), I won't (pay for your college).

I don't care what you think. *(impolite)*

9. Describing Feelings

Happiness

I'm doing great.

This is the best day of my life.

I've never been so happy in my life.

I'm so pleased for you.

Aren't you thrilled?

What could be better?

Life is good.

Sadness

Are you OK?

Why the long face?

I'm not doing so well.

I feel awful.

I'm devastated.

I'm depressed.

I'm feeling kind of blue.

I just want to crawl in a hole.

Oh, what's the use?

Fear

I'm worried about (money).

He dreads (going to the dentist).

I'm afraid to (drive over bridges).

She can't stand (snakes).

This anxiety is killing me.

He's scared of (big dogs).

How will I ever (pass Friday's test)?

I have a phobia about (germs).

Anger

I'm really mad at (you).
They resent (such high taxes).
How could she (do) that?
I'm annoyed with (the neighbors).
(The noise of car alarms) infuriates her.
He was furious with (the children).

Boredom

I'm so bored.
There's nothing to do around here.
What a bore!
Nothing ever happens.
She was bored to tears.
They were bored to death.
I was bored stiff.
It was such a monotonous (movie).
(That TV show) was so dull.

Disgust

That's disgusting.
Eeew! Yuck! *(informal)*
I hate (raw fish).
How can you stand it?
I almost vomited.
I thought I'd puke. *(impolite)*
I don't even like to think about it.
How can you say something like that?
I wouldn't be caught dead (wearing that dirty old coat).

Compassion

I'm sorry.
I understand what you're going through.
Tell me about it.
How can I help?
Is there anything I can do?
She is concerned about him.
He worries about (the children).
He cares for her deeply.
My heart goes out to them. *(old-fashioned)*

Guilt

I feel terrible that I (lost your mother's necklace).
I never should have (borrowed it).
I feel so guilty!
It's all my fault.
I blame myself.
I make a mess of everything.
I'll never forgive myself.

Photo Credits

Preliminary Chapter

Page x: Blue Jean Images/Alamy **Page 1:** Dean Mitchell/deanm1974/iStockphoto.com **Page 3:** Hill Street Studios/Blend Images/Alamy **Page 5:** top left Stockbroker/MBI/Alamy; second left allOver/TPH/Age Fotostock; third left David Grossman/Alamy; fourth left Mingzhe Zhang/iStockphoto.com; bottom Radius Images/Jupiter Images **Page 9:** Juanmonino/iStockphoto **Page 11:** Michael Doolittle/Alamy **Page 13:** Creatas Images/Jupiter Images **Page 14:** wavebreakmedia ltd/Shutterstock.com **Page 15:** Images.com/Alamy

Chapter 1

Page 16: Thomas Roetting/Age Fotostock **Page 17:** first left Realimage/Alamy; second left Daubigny's Garden, 1890 (oil on canvas), Gogh, Vincent van (1853–90)/Van Gogh Museum, Amsterdam, The Netherlands/Giraudon/The Bridgeman Art Library; third left lubilub/iStockphoto.com; fourth left Landscape with Rowboats 1916–18 (oil on canvas), Prendergast, Maurice Brazil (1858/9–1924)/The Barnes Foundation, Merion, Pennsylvania, USA/The Bridgeman Art Library; fifth left NASA Images; sixth left Alonistaina, Tripolis, 1958 (b/w photo), Tombazis, Nikolaos (1894–1986)/Benaki Museum, Athens, Greece/The Bridgeman Art Library **Page 18:** left Laurence Young; right Laurence Young **Page 19:** Mountain Village (Autumnal) 1934, (no 209) (oil on primed canvas on wooden panel), Klee, Paul (1879–1940)/GalerieRosengart, Lucerne, Switzerland/The Bridgeman Art Library **Page 22:** top Marcia Dalbey; bottom Marcia Dalbey **Page 25:** top Arlen Chlad/GoldenCreations/iStockphoto.com; center James Estrin/The New York Time/Redux Pictures **Page 27:** bottom left MarekUliasz/iStockphoto.com; bottom right Karen Struthers/karens4/istockphoto.com **Page 28:** center center ARENA Creative/Shutterstock.com; center top right Kuzma/Shutterstock.com; center left loraks/Shutterstock.com; center bottom right IlyaAndriyanov/Shutterstock.com; center bottom left CarstenReisinger/Shutterstock.com; center center wavebreakmedia ltd/Shutterstock.com **Page 29:** top left Laurence Young; top right Laurence Young; bottom left Laurence Young; bottom right Marcia Dalbey

Chapter 2

Page 30: kali9/iStockphoto.com **Page 32:** top left Ryerson Clark/iStockphoto.com; top right muratsarica/numbeos/iStockphoto.com; bottom left RyersonClark/iStockphoto.com; bottom right Marcelo Piotti/iStockphoto.com **Page 33:** top DNY59/iStockphoto.com; center Burrito/iStockphoto.com; bottom ivanastar/iStockphoto.com **Page 36:** Fancy/Veer/Corbis/Jupiter Images **Page 38:** left Christopher Futcher/CEFutcher/iStockphoto.com; center Blackbeck/iStockphoto.com; right Ryan McVay/Jupiter Images **Page 39:** top left mark wragg/wragg/iStockphoto.com; top right Scott Leigh/pastorscott/iStockphoto.com; bottom left Shawn Gearhart/ideabug/iStockphoto.com; bottom right Eneri LLC/Ceneri/iStockphoto.com

Page 40: Ryan Lane/iStockphoto.com **Page 43:** left pamspix/iStockphoto.com; center Chuck Schmidt/iStockphoto.com; right kevin miller/laughingmango/iStockphoto.com **Page 44:** top left Frances Twitty/ftwitty/iStockphoto.com; bottom left George Doyle/Jupiter Images; top right John Lund/Nevada Wier/Jupiter Images bottom center Jon Schulte/SchulteProductions/iStockphoto.com; bottom right Justin Horrocks/jhorrocks/iStockphoto.com

Chapter 3

Page 45: Radius Images/Alamy **Page 47:** top left Vstock/Alamy; top center Vibe Images/Alamy; top right Scott Vickers/iStockphoto.com; bottom left amana images inc./Alamy; bottom right Young-Wolff Photography/Alamy **Page 51:** Christopher Futcher/iStockphoto.com **Page 53:** top left cstar55/iStockphoto.com; top center Art of Food/Alamy; top right Paul Matthew Photography/Shutterstock.com; center left CagriÖzgür/iStockphoto.com; center center Oksana Struk/iStockphoto.com; center right GWImages/Shutterstock.com **Page 54:** coka/Shutterstock.com **Page 57:** PhotoEdit/Alamy **Page 58:** top Basheera Designs/Shutterstock.com; bottom R. Gino Santa Maria/Shutterstock.com

Chapter 4

Page 59: Kim Karpeles/Alamy **Page 60:** top left Pictor International/ImageState/Alamy; bottom right Rossario/Shutterstock.com **Page 61:** top Jeff Greenberg/Alamy; center left Tim Denison/jackscoldsweat/iStockphoto.com; center right RonTech2000/iStockphoto.com; bottom left Dieter Hawlan/iStockphoto.com; bottom right David Young-Wolff/PhotoEdit **Page 62:** bottom center Shyshak roman/Shutterstock.com; bottom right Yuri Arcurs/Shutterstock.com; top left Ostill/Shutterstock.com; top right Loskutnikov/Shutterstock.com; bottom left Robert Kneschke/Shutterstock.com **Page 63:** MorePixels/Photos.com **Page 65:** Suzanne Tucker/Shutterstock.com

Chapter 5

Page 73: Dean Mitchell/iStockphoto.com **Page 76:** top left Huntstock/the Agency Collection/Jupiter Images; center Andresr/Shutterstock.com **Page 78:** Alexander Raths/iStockphoto.com **Page 83:** Lisa F. Young/iStockphoto.com **Page 84:** AwakenedEye/iStockphoto.com **Page 86:** microgen/iStockphoto.com **Page 87:** Photo Researchers, Inc/Photo Researchers **Page 88:** REDAV/Shutterstock.com

Chapter 6

Page 89: Dennis Hallinan/Alamy **Page 90:** top left fr73/istockphoto.com; top right kdow/iStockphoto.com; second left konstantin32/iStockphoto.com;second right iofoto/Shutterstock; center left John

Alves/Danita Delimont/Alamy; center right LPETTET/iStockphoto.com; fourth left egdigital/iStockphoto.com; fourth right KingWu/iStockphoto.com; bottom left Jo Ann Snover/iStockphoto.com; bottom right Karl Buhl/Danita Delimont/Alamy Limited **Page 92:** top lolloj/Shutterstock.com; bottom Christopher Futcher/iStockphoto.com **Page 93:** dbtravel/dbimages/Alamy **Page 94:** Universal Images Group Limited/Alamy **Page 99:** Jeff Greenberg/Alamy **Page 104:** top left Meunierd/Shutterstock.com; top center Wollwerth/DreamstimeLLC; top right Djembe/Dreamstime LLC; bottom left Wollwerth/Dreamstime LLC; bottom center Ranplett/iStockphoto.com; bottom right Meunierd/Shutterstock.com

Chapter 7

Page 106: Jeff Greenberg/Alamy **Page 109:** Francisblack/iStockphoto.com **Page 110:** nastia11/Shutterstock.com **Page 114:** left stefanolunardi/Shutterstock.com; right Radius Images/

Jupiter Images **Page 115:** Rich Legg/iStockphoto.com **Page 116:** SilviaJansen/iStockphoto.com **Page 117:** Editorial/Alamy **Page 119:** Americanspirit/Dreamstime LLC **Page 122:** Zurijeta/Shutterstock.com

Chapter 8

Page 123: Stockbyte/Jupiter Images **Page 126:** top Rich Legg/iStockphoto.com; bottom kristian sekulic/iStockphoto.com **Page 127:** Aaron Amat/Shutterstock.com **Page 130:** left Tony Tremblay/iStockphoto.com; center boyan1971/Shutterstock.com; right Andrey Bayda/Shutterstock.com **Page 132:** Ersler Dmitry/Shutterstock.com **Page 133:** Baloncici/Shutterstock.com **Page 134:** Joakim Carlgren/iStockphoto.com **Page 135:** Diego Cervo/Shutterstock.com **Page137:** FlashonStudio/Shutterstock.com **Page 138:** HultonArchive/iStockphoto.com